The Craftsman's Art Series

The Craft of
Woodwork

Roy Day

Stanley Paul, London

Dimensions in this book are quoted in both metric and
imperial units.

Metrication has affected some tool dimensions
and their nomenclature. Remaining at their established sizes
some, such as wood screws, have continued to use the imperial
measurements and gauges, so that metrication has involved only
a straight conversion of numbers. Other tools whose quoted
dimensions need not be exact have adopted nominal metric
equivalents – for example hammers, saws and cramps – and
have not undergone straight conversion. Metrication has
resulted in some tools (including nails) being manufactured to
new metric British Standards.

Stanley Paul & Co Ltd
3 Fitzroy Square, London W1

An Imprint of the Hutchinson Publishing Group

London Melbourne Sydney Auckland
Wellington Johannesburg and agencies
throughout the world

First published 1976
© Roy Day 1976
Illustrations © Stanley Paul & Co Ltd 1976

Printed in Great Britain by The Anchor Press Ltd
and bound by Wm Brendon & Son Ltd, both of
Tiptree, Essex

ISBN 0 09 124800 0 (cased)
      0 09 124801 9 (paperback)

Contents

I. Materials

If you are new to woodworking you are faced immediately with a three-sided quandary. Which materials should you buy, which tools from the vast array will you need, and finally, is it possible for a beginner to make a piece of furniture that will be a useful and pleasing addition to a room?

The answer to the last question is yes. The fact that you are reading this book means that you are interested in starting woodwork. That interest implies that, deep down, you believe you have the ability to work with your hands – even if only at a simple level.

With a minimum of ability most people should, with care, be able to produce a passable first effort – aesthetically and technically. From then on improvement will be linked to experience.

The basic tools in a woodworking kit – saw, hammer, screwdriver and so on – will be found in most households. Using these on scrap pieces of wood will enable you to judge whether or not you will be able to master the basic techniques covered in this book. Later on it will be worth supplementing the basic tools with more specialized items which will make your woodworking achievements more enjoyable and successful.

Advising individuals on how much to pay for a tool kit is difficult since so much depends on the individual pocket. Cheap tools are rarely cheap, because invariably they have to be replaced – and usually this is sooner rather than later. Good tools, properly cared for, will last a lifetime, proving that old adage that the most expensive is usually the cheapest in the long run.

How do you choose the materials with which to do the job?

Through the advent of man-made boards, woodworkers are no longer restricted to timber as a constructional material. Additional names to conjure with nowadays include 'chipboard', 'blockboard' and a range of 'veneered' boards. These modern materials, all of which are readily available from timber merchants and many do-it-yourself (d-i-y) shops, are geared towards making life a lot easier and they do just that provided that you know how to work them and use them.

You must have a basic knowledge of the construction and qualities of both timber and man-made boards. This will enable you to select the right material for the job. Knowing how materials can be used means that the most economical method can be chosen to achieve the same end result. For example, a side panel of a cupboard could be constructed more cheaply from softwood battens covered with a sheet of hardboard than from a piece of chipboard. On the other hand, there will be those who will be prepared to sacrifice economy for simplicity and speed by using chipboard. In other situations where for example, strength or decorative appearance is important, certain materials will not be suitable.

2. Timber

This section will help you sort out which material to use for which job.

Hard- or softwood?

Trees are divided into two groups, coniferous and deciduous. Coniferous trees, from which softwoods come, are evergreens distinguishable by their needle-like leaves. Deciduous trees, from which hardwoods come, have broad leaves which fall off in the autumn.

Although, in the main, hardwoods *are* harder than softwoods, this is not a strict rule. There are exceptions. Balsa, for example, though classified as a hardwood, is soft and easy to work, whereas pitch pine is classified as a softwood and yet is hard to work. However, for basic purposes, the descriptions can be accepted and used as a guide.

Softwoods are cheaper than hardwoods. This is because all deciduous trees (hardwoods) are grown in the temperate regions of the world where timber takes longer to mature. There are fewer forests of deciduous trees, but a greater variety of species. Therefore there are many more types of hardwoods.

Coniferous trees (softwood) grow in great forests tightly packed with tall trees, usually of the same species. This makes it easier to harvest and transport the timber to the sawmills and then to the timber yards. Therefore, being in plentiful supply and easily obtainable, softwoods are cheaper.

Hardwoods are heavy, more varied, tougher to work, durable and often have an attractive colour and grain formation. Softwoods are lighter, easy to work with simple equipment and light coloured.

Most handymen work with softwood because it is economical.

How to choose good wood

As soon as a tree is cut down it is taken to the sawmill to be cut into usable sizes – planks, boards and squares.

Plain sawn is the quickest method. There is little waste and therefore this is also the least expensive method. However, although the boards cut from the middle of the log will not warp, those cut towards the outside will warp outwards when the wood dries out.

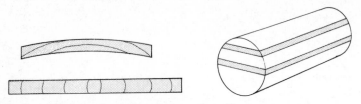

Boards cut from the middle of the tree are unlikely to warp. Those cut towards the outside will be more inclined to warp when the wood dries out.

Some woods have particularly decorative surfaces and this is revealed by quarter sawing. This is the most expensive method and also produces boards which are far less likely to warp.

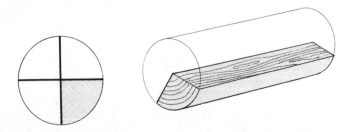

Boards which are quarter sawn will reveal a particularly decorative surface ideal for the most attractively grained timber. Although an expensive method of sawing it will produce boards which are far less likely to warp.

When choosing timber it pays to study the direction of the annual rings. Each ring, or layer of wood, represents one year's growth. If the rings run from edge to edge across the width of the board it means that the board has been flat sawn. If the rings run from side to side across the thickness of the board, the board has been quarter sawn.

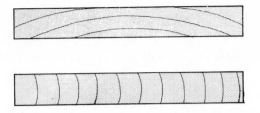

If the rings run from edge to edge across the cut end of the board — the board has been flat sawn.
If the rings run across the thickness of the board at the sawn end — it has been quarter sawn.

After it has been sawn up the timber must be partially dried or seasoned making it more durable, and easier to work. Unseasoned wood is weaker, more likely to warp, harder to work, and is more likely to attract fungus.

The moisture content in wood must be equal to its surroundings otherwise it will shrink or swell. For example, the moisture content of a room is 16 per cent; therefore the moisture content of a new door must be 16 per cent.

So, if the moisture content of a room is 16 per cent and the moisture content of the new door is only 10 per cent, the door will swell as it absorbs more moisture to bring it up to 16 per cent.

However, if the moisture content of the new door is 20 per cent, then the door will shrink as it loses some moisture to bring it down to 16 per cent.

This is what happens in a house when the doors stick in the winter yet open freely in the summer.

When buying timber always ask how it has been seasoned. Two methods are used to season new timber: kiln drying and air drying.

Kiln drying is a quick process. It reduces the moisture content of the timber to about 10 per cent. This is the required percentage for timber which is to be used in a centrally heated house. However, as kiln dried timber is expensive and difficult to obtain, many people will have no choice but to use air dried timber.

Air drying is a slower process and can only reduce the moisture content of wood to about 16 per cent. So it should be seasoned for a second time by standing it for a few weeks in the room where it is to be used.

Do not stand timber in the open air for a long time before use. It will soak up rainwater, thus increasing the moisture content.

Defects

The past history of a tree – its growth, felling and seasoning – sets up stresses that can affect the strength and appearance of the finished article. So it pays to look out for certain defects when buying stock at the timber yard.

Most of the common faults are cut out of timber before it reaches the timber yard, but knots, shakes, waney edge, resin pockets and sapwood are often present. These defects vary in quantity with the grade of the timber.

Knots, the cross sections of branches, are usually only found in softwoods. They weaken the timber. If a knot is 'live' it will be sound, tight, will feel slightly sticky with resin, and is not a great defect. Sometimes a knot can be used deliberately in an article as a decorative feature. A dead knot feels dry, will be loose or will already have fallen out.

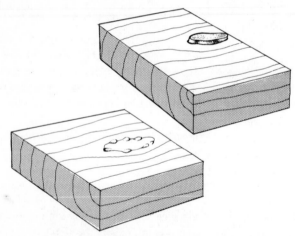

If a knot is 'live' it will be sound and tight and might be slightly sticky with resin.
A 'dead' knot may be loose or have already have fallen out. It will not be sticky with resin and might possibly be black in colour.

Shakes (or splits as they are sometimes called) vary. *Heart* shakes are the result of decay at the centre of the tree which has spread outwards. *Star* shakes are caused when timber is dried more rapidly on the outside than in the middle. *Felling* shakes occur when the tree crashes to the ground. These are indicated by cracks across the grain.

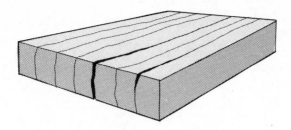

'Shakes' can occur anywhere across a board and appear in the form of splits. These are usually caused by rapid drying of the timber.

A waney edge is found on the last piece of timber cut from a tree. Often a piece of bark may still be attached. A waney edge is more prone to attack from decay and insects. If you have to use a plank with a waney edge, then work well inside the edge.

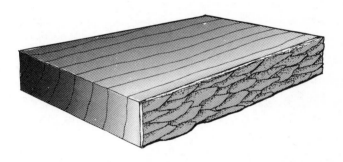

Waney edge is the outer section of the tree which appears at one side of the board and often includes a piece of bark. The sapwood inside the bark shows as a discoloured band which is more prone to decay and insect attack.

Resin pockets are small pockets of resin which may become apparent only after the wood has been planed. If a pocket is on a surface which is to be painted or varnished, the resin should be scraped away and the resinous area coated with an application of shellac knotting. The resultant depression can then be levelled off with a wood filler. If this is not done, the resin will work through to the surface and spoil the finish.

Sapwood

Do not accept hardwood boards which have lighter colour strips down the edges. This is part of the sapwood and is less durable and harder to stain than timber of uniform colour.

Discoloration of a complete board occurs when the timber has been stored in the open. This is not serious since, usually, it can be planed back to bright timber. Where discoloration cannot be removed, the timber is quite suitable for structural work but do not use it where you want a decorative finish.

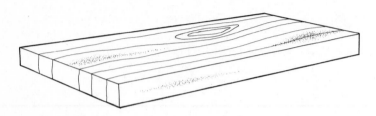

Some discoloration can occur on healthy timber due to being stored in the open. Although quite sound for structural work, this should not be accepted as a decorative finish.

Quantities

For some time now, timber has been sold in metric dimensions. Metres (m) replace feet for length and millimetres (mm) replace inches for sections.

As you will see from the table (on page 91), softwood lengths start at 1·8 m and increase in 300 mm stages to 6'3 m; 300 mm is slightly less than 1 ft.

Thicknesses range from 16 mm to 300 mm, and widths from 75 mm to 300 mm.

All dimensions can be converted to the old imperial measure on the basis of 25 mm equals 1 in. (see table). If you continue to work out dimensions in imperial measure, then round up the measurements to the nearest metric size available.

However, with practice, it is easier and more economical to calculate in metric measurements since you will be charged for the wasted timber.

Timber is available in sawn sizes and planed sizes. A raw length of timber is sawn to an exact size by the timber yard, for example, 75 mm (3 in) thick. However, to give it a smooth finish, it is then planed. The planing removes about 3 mm ($\frac{1}{8}$ in) of timber from each side of the length of wood, making a total of 6 mm ($\frac{1}{4}$ in) on the complete width.

The sizes quoted are the sawn sizes (referred to as the nominal sizes) and are therefore misleading. A 75 mm (3 in) wide (nominal

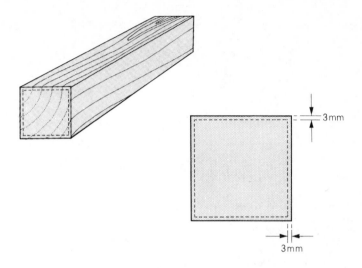

3 mm

3 mm

Timber is sawn to the exact dimension for example 75 mm × 75 mm (3 ins × 3 ins). Planed or prepared timber has had up to 3 mm ($\frac{1}{8}$ in) removed from each face giving a finished size of 70 mm × 70 mm. (Note that this is still referred to as 75 mm × 75 mm, or 3 ins × 3 ins, prepared timber).

size) section is in fact nearer 70 mm ($2\frac{3}{4}$ ins) wide when planed. The planed size is called the 'finished' size.

So, if you design some shelves, for example, and they are to be 150 mm (6 ins) wide then specify to your supplier that this is the finished size. If you do not then the shelves will be only 145 mm ($5\frac{3}{4}$ ins) wide which could be critical.

Remember, too, that each batch of timber supplied by a timber merchant can vary slightly in its finished dimensions depending on the mill from which it was bought.

Chipboard

This is made from compressed wood shavings mixed with a synthetic resin glue. These are bonded together under heat and pressure.

Chipboard is priced according to its density; the boards with the highest density are the best grades. The most popular thicknesses vary from about 12 mm ($\frac{1}{2}$ in) to 18 mm ($\frac{3}{4}$ in).

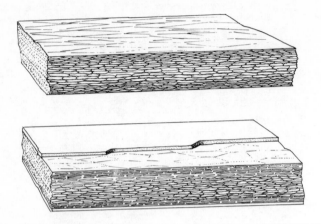

Chipboard is available in plain finish in a range of thicknesses. The most common is 12 mm and 18 mm. It is also available faced with a range of veneers or a plastic finish.

Chipboard is sold with either a plain or veneered surface, or with a hard, patterned plastic surface. It is fairly stable and uniform in shape and size. It can be worked with basic hand tools, though it would blunt an ordinary saw quickly because of the high resin content of the board.

Screws must not be overtightened or they will lose their holding power. Special chipboard screws which have a coarse thread are available.

It is not a structurally sound material, however, so it should not be used without plenty of support if it is expected to carry a lot of weight. However, it can be used for doors or similar jobs which will not put it under strain.

The surface of the plain chipboard is pitted so it must be filled before painting. If you pay a little more you can buy a board which is ready for immediate painting.

There are certain veneered boards on the market, which are ideal for furniture-making. These are sold in standard panel sizes which are veneered along all edges. A little skill can produce a professional job here as long as a unit of furniture can be designed to suit standard sizes, thus eliminating sawing off a veneered edge to reveal the core of the board.

However, since the board is heavy, larger units should be permanent, fitted structures which never have to be moved. Smaller units could be fitted with castors for mobility.

Blockboard

This is made from strips of softwood which are laid end to end and then sandwiched between sheets of veneer, often of birch. It is more expensive than chipboard as it tends to be more stable. The standard of manufacture is not always high, however, which limits its uses. Often some of the softwood strips are missing or loose and the covering veneer may be peeling away.

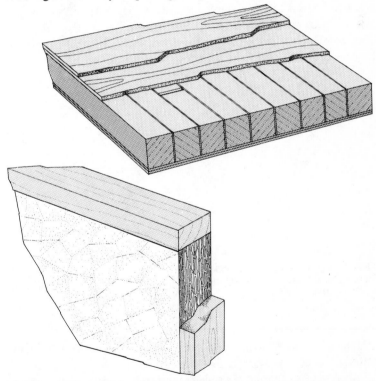

Blockboard is made from strips of softwood sandwiched between sheets of plywood veneer, often birch. The common thickness is 18 mm. Like chipboard sheets are 8 ft × 4 ft or the nearest metric equivalent.

Exposed edges of boards can be covered with a lipping material – usually hardwood – to hide the unattractive structure of the board.

However, a well-made section can be used for doors, table tops, shelving, room dividers and so on. The edges can be covered with a lipping material to hide the unattractive construction.

Laminboard is of the same construction as blockboard but is better quality and therefore much more expensive.

Hardboard

Hardboard is the cheapest man-made board and is manufactured from softwood pulp pressed into sheets which can be as much as 12 mm ($\frac{1}{2}$ in) thick though the commonly used thickness is 3 mm ($\frac{1}{8}$ in). The standard sheets have one smooth face and one rough textured face.

Hardboard bends easily but will not warp. It is used mainly as a cladding material over a framework of battens. The soft edges can be damaged easily if knocked, so in situations where this is likely to happen, such as flush panelling for doors, it is advisable to protect the edges by covering them with a lipping material.

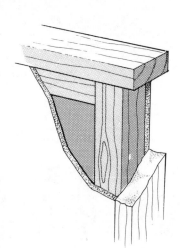

Always lip or frame up hardboard to protect the soft edge which will fray if left exposed.

Hardboard is easy to work and is an ideal base for finishing materials since it provides a fairly good surface.

Other types of hardboard include tempered board, which is more water resistant. This comes in the same thickness as standard hardboard. Panelboard, a less dense type, has fewer uses but it could be fixed in a child's room as a pin-up board.

Hardboard with lots of evenly spaced holes on the surface is

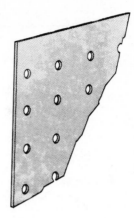

Standard hardboard 3 mm ($\frac{1}{8}$ in) thick, will bend easily. Pegboard is a standard hardboard with evenly spaced holes drilled through it. It is an ideal covering material where ventilation is required.

commonly called pegboard. This is ideal as a covering material where ventilation is required. Or it could be used as a simple kitchen clip-up board.

Plywood

Timber sheets are glued, under pressure, with their grain at right angles to each other to form plywood. Plywood is graded according to the quality of the veneers and adhesive used in manufacture.

Where three layers of veneer are used, the board is called 3 ply; five veneers are called 5 ply. Where more than five veneers are used, the board is called multi-ply.

The crossbonding of the veneers gives the board more strength and stability. Plywood has many uses including cladding over battens to provide an excellent surface for a decorative covering, or for such things as drawer bottoms.

The thicker boards, 12 mm ($\frac{1}{2}$ in) or 18 mm ($\frac{3}{4}$ in), can be joined together to make cabinet sides and suchlike, but this would be a costly method on a par with using blockboard.

Moisture-resisting plywood can be used outdoors. This exterior grade type is identified by the letters WBP on the label. This means it is water- and boilproof.

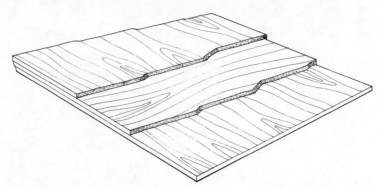

Plywood is graded according to the number of veneers used, 3 ply, 5 ply or multiply. The crossbonding of the veneers give the boards strength and stability.

Man-made boards or timber?

Man-made boards are preferable to natural timber because:

They are available in large sheets 2440 mm × 1220 mm (8 ft × 4 ft) which can be cut up into the required sizes.

With careful designing, veneered boards can be simply joined together to make professional furniture.

They are less likely to warp or shrink.

Where panels of over 305 mm (1 ft) wide are needed they are more economical.

They provide a better weight/strength ratio.

However:

Their inability to withstand heavy loads over longer distances limits their use.

Some need special edge treatment (lipping or veneering) to hide an unattractive appearance.

With the exception of WBP plywood they can only be used inside the house since they readily absorb moisture.

3. Basic Operations

This section shows you how to set about some of the basic operations in woodworking and how to use the tools that go with them: rules and try squares for accurate marking, planes, saws, chisels, hammers, drills, screws and G cramps.

The rule

Measuring and marking must be completely accurate. This means that such things as a cloth tape used for dressmaking is not suitable because it can stretch and wrinkle and will distort measurements.

Even metal tapes can kink or twist but one of these, used with care, will do. The extendable types, often over 1·830 mm (6 ft) long, are especially handy for marking out large pieces of wood before cutting and planing.

A folded boxwood rule is the ideal. Use this standing on its edge so that the pencil mark will then be made exactly on line with the

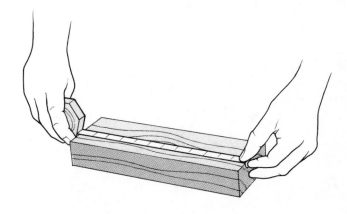

Use a metal tape — a 6 ft tape is ideal — or a folding boxwood rule for accurate measuring.

required mark on the rule. You will be liable to make mistakes if the rule is laid flat: the pencil mark could be made slightly in front or behind the required point. Slight errors are not likely to be critical on a shelf or a table top, but on something such as a bookcase, a 2 mm ($\frac{1}{16}$ in) error made each time will build up into a sizeable gap.

The marking pencil must always have a sharp point, so keep a sharpener handy while you work – and use it often.

Squareness

Squareness is the basis of successful woodworking. In any assembly, every piece of wood must be square both individually and in relation to the others.

Do not be frightened of the term 'squareness'. It simply means that each corner of a piece of wood must be at right angles. Also, when two pieces of wood are fixed together, they must join at right angles (90 degrees) to each other.

A wonky cupboard door, a shelf that does not sit properly on its bearers, a wobbly table are more often than not caused by an assembly which is out of square.

Try square

A try square checks individual pieces of wood and small assemblies for squareness. A 150 mm (6 in) long try square is perfectly adequate for the beginner who is interested only in elementary work. A longer try square will show up more clearly any faults on larger pieces of wood.

It is worth while buying a good try square and taking care of it. The blade must be really firm in the handle – adjustment is never necessary.

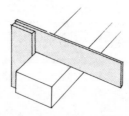

A try square checks individual pieces of wood and small assemblies for squareness. A 150 mm (6 in) long square is adequate for the beginner.

Never assume that timber brought at a timber yard or a d-i-y shop is square, unless, of course, you specifically asked, and possibly paid, for it to be planed square. Even then it is always worth while double-checking when you get home. Man-made boards must be checked similarly.

It is unlikely that a saw cut will leave a square corner irrespective of how carefully you marked and cut it. So always go through the squaring up process (see page 23) with individual pieces of timber. This may sound laborious, but it is absolutely essential.

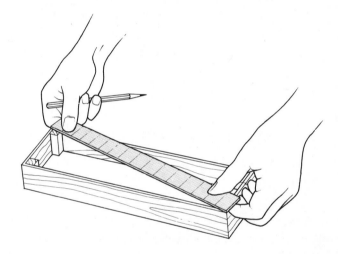

For large assemblies squareness can be checked by measuring across the diagonals. If the two measurements are identical the assembly is square.

Although the try square can be used to test small assemblies, an alternative is to measure across the diagonals. If they are exactly the same, the assembly is square.

A marking gauge

This is used to scribe a line parallel to a true edge.

The stock of the gauge slides along the stem and is locked in the required position by tightening the thumb screw. The required position is ascertained by holding the gauge to a rule.

The scriber must not be pushed deeply into the wood. This will

A marking gauge is used to scribe a parallel line to a true edge of a piece of timber. The scribing point must not be pushed too deeply into the surface of the wood.

merely make it wander along the grain line. It must be pushed along gently. Push the stock of the gauge firmly against a true edge. This will keep the scriber on a true course.

Mark only a short distance at a time. After each stroke, roll the gauge forward so that the scriber leaves the surface.

A makeshift marking gauge can be made with a steel rule and a pencil.

Squaring a piece of wood

First, test one side for smoothness. If you can see daylight under the inverted blade of the try square then the high spots will have to be planed down.

This can be done only by taking off shavings in easy stages. Plane a little – check, plane a little – check, and so on until the face is perfectly smooth. Test at several points along the length.

Test the length or wider pieces of timber with a steel straight-edge. Never trust a wood straight-edge.

Mark the first smooth face to show that it has been worked on.

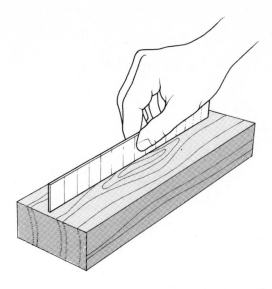

Test the length or wide pieces of timber for level by using a steel straight edge.

Next, check one of the edges that forms a right angle with the marked face. The angle must be a perfect 90 degrees and the second side must be perfectly smooth.

Push the handle of the try square flat against the workpiece and look for daylight under the blade. Test several points along the length. Take off any high spots as before.

Set the marking gauge to the required thickness. Push the stock firmly against one of the smooth sides. Draw the cutting edge down the length until the required line is completely marked. Do this on both sides of the workpiece to give a line to plane down to. Finally, test the second side for squareness and plane down as necessary.

Squaring an end

To square an end of a workpiece, hold the stock of the try square firmly against either the face side or face edge of the workpiece. Draw a pencil line along the blade.

Work right around the workpiece in the same way until you have a continuous line marked on all four faces.

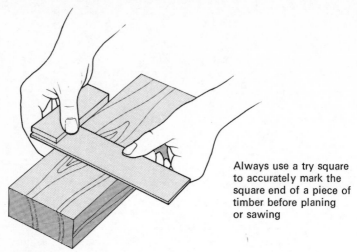

Always use a try square
to accurately mark the
square end of a piece of
timber before planing
or sawing

Planing

A plane smoothes timber and reduces it to the exact size required.

If you are a complete beginner you will find a small block plane the most useful. This is shaped so that it can be held easily in one hand while working which makes it easier to use than one of the larger, longer types. Its size, however, does limit its usefulness. It is adequate only for smoothing shorter pieces of timber, end grain and edges. On longer timbers it will tend to dip into the surface and do more harm than good.

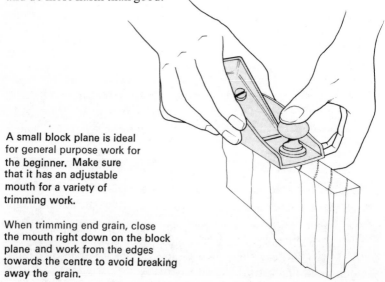

A small block plane is ideal
for general purpose work for
the beginner. Make sure
that it has an adjustable
mouth for a variety of
trimming work.

When trimming end grain, close
the mouth right down on the block
plane and work from the edges
towards the centre to avoid breaking
away the grain.

A jack plane, about 375 mm (15 in) long, is made for the true smoothing of longer surfaces. Its length prevents it dipping into any hollows in the timber surface. However it is not much use for end grain. The blade of the jack plane is slightly curved, thus the edges will not leave score marks on the surface of the timber.

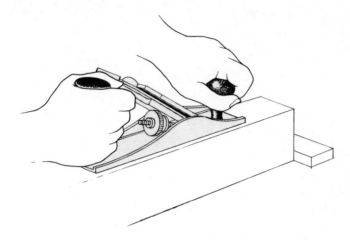

A smoothing plane or jack plane is ideal for smoothing longer lengths of timber. But it is not suitable for trimming end grain where far more skill is required.

A plane has to be set correctly according to the amount of wood needed to be removed. It is far easier to adjust the cutting iron (blade) of a metal plane to the depth and evenness of the required cut. Usually, all adjustments are made with a knob and lever. Wooden planes are much more difficult to set correctly.

When you buy a plane, the iron will be something less than sharp. This is deliberately done to prevent accidents on the plane's journey from the factory to your workbox. This means that either you have to sharpen it yourself (see page 40) or ask the shop to do it for you. Since, however, it will need to be kept constantly sharp, it is better to learn to do this yourself.

You can avoid the bother of sharpening a plane by buying a ready-sharpened replaceable blade plane. When blunt, the old blade is discarded and a new one fitted in seconds.

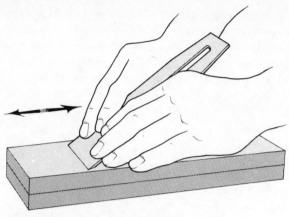

Like new chisels new planes are supplied with a blade which has a lacquered ground edge. This will require honing on an oil stone to form a secondary cutting edge.

The Stanley Surform can be recommended to anyone who does not regard the home of a plane as being only in a woodwork kit. It is not a plane in the conventional sense, but is very useful for any general work where precision is not a key factor. Its advantages are that its versatility allows you to cut curves and other clever woodworking shapes, and it can also be used on soft metals and a host of

The Surform plane is ideal for trimming back rough sawn timber. It will not achieve the same degree of smoothness on finished timber as a conventional plane. Several shapes and sizes of Surform are available for flat and curved trimming. All blades are replaceable.

other materials. So if your plane has to do service all round the house, garage and garden, then this could be a better buy.

Blades incidentally, are replaceable. Just slip out the old and click on the new.

Adjusting the blade

You will soon develop an eye for correct plane blade adjustment. Look along the sole (the base) with the plane held at eye level. The projecting edge of the iron must be parallel with the sole. The distance that it projects determines the depth of cut. The knob adjusts the projection; the lever takes care of lateral adjustment.

Practise on waste wood until you get used to knowing how much the iron takes off when in different positions. Ideally it should work with very little effort to remove smooth shavings.

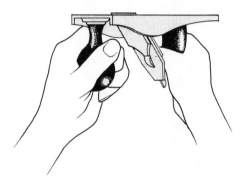

When adjusting a plane look along the sole – the base – once the blade has been sharpened. The distance it projects determines the depth of cut.

Using the plane

It is always difficult for a beginner to appreciate terms like 'let the body do the work'. However, when you get into the swing of planing you will find, as everyone does, that the following technique is the best and most natural.

Throughout each stroke, the plane must remain horizontal otherwise you will get an uneven cut. Start by pressing down on the front knob, putting all your weight on the front foot. As you move the plane across the surface, gradually transfer your weight on to the other foot and increase pressure on the back of the plane.

Planing end grain

A block plane equipped with an adjustable mouth is the ideal for planing end grain. With the adjustable mouth closed down to the smallest aperture, the tool will be set correctly to tackle this job. The danger when planing end grain is that a corner of the workpiece might chip or splinter.

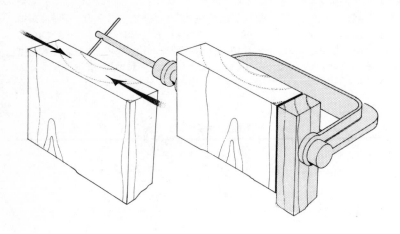

Alternatively clamp a small piece of wood flush to the finishing end to avoid damaging it.

One of two techniques can be used to avoid chipping. Either plane to the centre of the wood, working from each end, or clamp a spare piece of wood flush with the finishing end to leave a 'continuous surface'.

Man-made boards, especially the largest sheets, can be awkward to handle. Secure them with a couple of kitchen stools, chairs or trestles.

Mark the pencil guide-line clearly and finely. A thick pencil line can cause inaccuracies. You will be surprised at how much timber is removed from both sides of the saw, so never cut on the pencil line, otherwise the workpiece will end up a fraction shorter than intended.

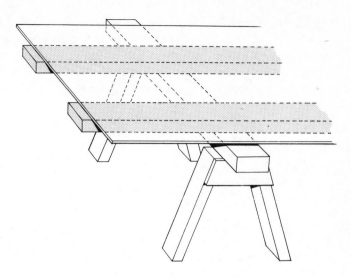

Large boards of plywood or chipboard should be well supported along both edges before proceeding to saw through them. Failure to do this will result in the board tearing due to its heavy weight.

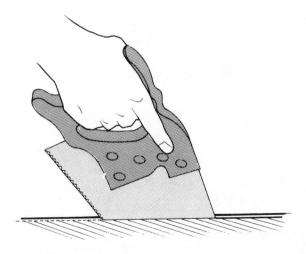

Remember that 1·5 mm ($\frac{1}{16}$ in) or more will be lost on the saw cut. Mark the cutting line boldly in pencil and saw slightly to the waste side – the side to be removed from the finished piece.

Make the cut on the waste side of the wood. It is easy to forget which is the waste side, so scribble a few pencil crosses on it after marking the guide-line.

When nearing the end of a cut, support the waste side of the wood to prevent it dropping away. If it does this it will splinter the good side as it tears off.

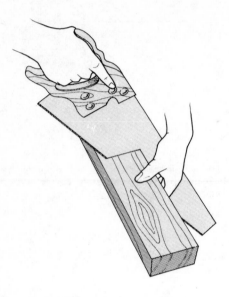

Always try to support the waste piece of timber especially at the final cutting stroke to prevent tearing.

You will need a helper to support the waste side of large panels.

When making the last few cuts, work lightly and slowly, again to avoid tearing.

Occasionally, especially on long cuts, the saw may get stuck. This sometimes happens because the saw has twisted slightly through being forced back into a straight line. In this case, ease it out and start cutting again from the other end.

One sure way to prevent sticking is to knock a small timber wedge into the beginning of the cut. This will prevent the wood closing up and trapping the blade again.

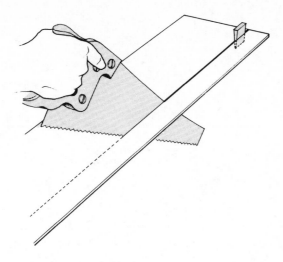

A small wedge inserted into the saw cut at the starting end when sawing along the length of timber will prevent the saw blade from being gripped too tightly as it progresses along the sawing line.

Sawing

Since wood has to be cut in both directions – with and across the grain – and also in shapes, curves, holes in the centre of a workpiece, and so on, there are many different types of saw made to facilitate individual operations.

However, since at first you are only likely to be sawing in a straight line then you will cope very well with a handsaw. This is sometimes called a panel saw. It will cut both with and across the grain.

If you already own a saw then the odds are it will be a 500 mm (20 in) or 550 mm (22 in) long handsaw anyway.

If the saw is one of these lengths, the support that you use for the workpiece should be about this height above the ground. This will prevent the blade touching the floor as you work.

The workpiece must be supported firmly and held down securely. If it is free to vibrate unduly, or move about, then easy, accurate sawing becomes difficult and can also cause accidents.

Never try to saw off narrow sections, say 12 mm ($\frac{1}{2}$ in) or less. Use the plane for a neat finish.

When marking out sections across a large panel, remember to take into account the width of the saw cut. For instance, you will not be able to cut four 710 mm (2 ft) wide panels from a 2440 mm

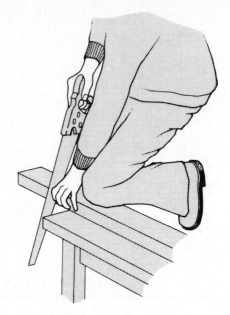

A 500 mm (20 in) or 550 mm (22 in) panel saw is ideal for general purpose work.

When using a saw make certain that the timber is held firmly either in a vice or with the combination of hand and knee. The saw blade should have room to travel the full extension of the blade through the timber.

(8 ft) sheet of hardboard, blockboard or whatever. The last section will be only about 605 mm (1 ft 11⅞ in).

A bench hook is useful when cutting small pieces of wood.

The cutting action

Gripping the saw handle correctly is a more or less natural reaction to the contours of the handle. The index finger, though, must point directly down the handle. This helps both to guide and control the saw.

Stand so that your eye, hand and shoulder are all in line with the saw blade. However, if you find that you can work more comfortably and accurately in some other position or stance, then use it.

The marked guide-line must be kept in view and not be hidden behind the saw, so arrange the workpiece accordingly.

Draw the kerf (the back of the cutting edge) of the saw backwards a few times to make a small indentation in the edge of the workpiece. This will prevent the saw from jumping out of its correct position as you start.

Saws only cut on the downward stroke so use a long, steady action using all the teeth, not just a few in the middle.

Do not apply any pressure as you draw the saw back towards you. Keep the saw at an angle of 45 degrees to the workpiece.

Sawing in a straight line

Only practise will help you to keep to a straight line. When sawing across a veneered face board, score a deep line with a sharp knife

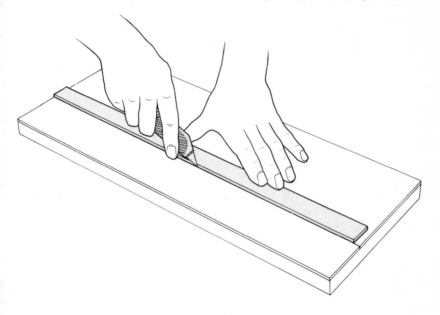

When sawing a veneered board, first score around all sides of the cutting line with a sharp knife; this will prevent the grain from tearing along the underside. It will also help to keep the saw at a shallow angle.

around the edges and faces to leave a furrow for the saw to follow (this will prevent splintering the edge of man-made boards). Always use a fine toothed saw when cutting veneered boards.

Remember, though, a blunt saw could be the problem, so get it sharpened professionally. A hardpoint saw of toughened steel

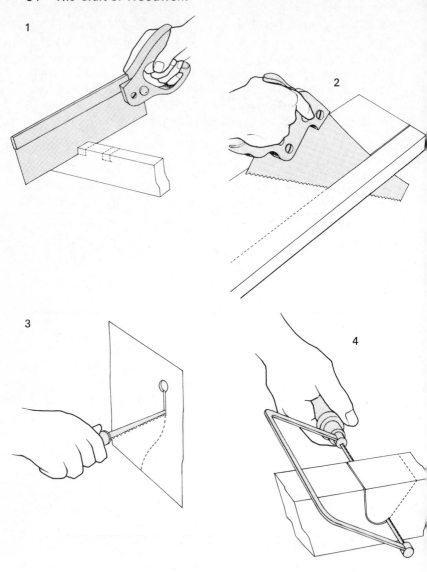

1 A 250 mm (10 in) or 300 mm (12 in) tenon saw is the first addition
  that should be made to your tool kit. Ideal for all joint cutting and accurate
  fine sawing.

2 A rip saw is ideal for cutting down the length of timber with the grain.

3 A pad saw is used for cutting a hole in a piece of timber. The narrow
  blade is inserted through a previously drilled pilot hole.

4 The coping saw is used for cutting gentle curves with accuracy. The
  bow saw and fret saw are variations of the coping saw.

is worth considering as it will remain sharp far longer than the conventional saw blade.

Other types of saw

Other saws, which are worth bearing in mind for future reference, should you develop into a woodworking enthusiast, are the tenon, rip, pad, bow and coping saws.

For cutting curves in a piece of timber 12 mm ($\frac{1}{2}$ in thick) or more use a bow saw. This consists of a narrow blade stretched tight in a wooden frame. The important thing in use is never to force the blade otherwise it will wander off line and could well break.

The coping saw is a smaller version of the bow saw and is used on thinner wood. The blade is adjustable, fixed in a steel frame.

For cutting a hole from the middle of a piece of wood, a hole must be drilled first for the saw blade to be threaded through. Fix the blade to the frame then sawing can begin. Obviously the size of the frame limits the distance from the edge of the wood that a hole can be cut.

A pad saw is invaluable for cutting holes in the middle of large panels, Again a hole has to be drilled for the blade to be inserted before sawing can begin.

A rip saw cuts with the grain of the wood. Its advantage over the basic handsaw for this work is that it is longer (about 650 mm or 26 in) and has sharper teeth, thus making the work a lot easier – and faster.

When you progress to the stage where you are producing more sophisticated work involving cutting accurate, complicated joints, then you will need a tenon saw. The usual size is 300 mm (12 in) or 350 mm (14 ins).

I have not mentioned power saws deliberately. Obviously these make the going easier, but since their expense can be justified only by the amount of work they will receive, they are not a sound initial investment for the beginner.

Chiselling

Chisels are needed extensively in advanced woodworking where, for example, they are used for cutting out sophisticated joints.

A chisel has simpler uses, however. The beginner will find it handy for paring a corner of a shelf to give it a rounded, decorative finish. It is used also for taking off a sliver of wood to make something fit. It is essential when cutting slots for door hinges.

For all basic work such as this, buy a bevelled edge firmer chisel. It gets its name from the shape of the blade which has the two long edges ground away. It is lighter and simpler to use than a firmer chisel or a mortice chisel, which are the most effective on robust work demanding a blade that will withstand heavier leverage.

The chisel size is denoted by the width of the blade. A couple

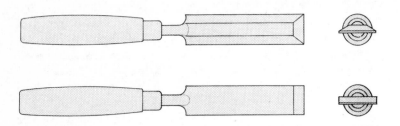

Bevelled edge chisels are ideal for general purpose work. Use the firmer chisels where more leverage is required such as cutting mortices. For the beginner one $\frac{1}{4}$ in (6 mm) and one 1 in (25 mm) are ideal.

of chisels, say $\frac{1}{4}$ in (6 mm) and 1 in (125 mm) wide, will suit you to begin with.

There are several more widths available up to $1\frac{1}{2}$ ins (38 mm) wide. The advantage of having a variety of sizes is that a strip of wood of a required width can be chopped out accurately in one go by selecting the right size chisel. Basic work, however, can be tackled successfully with a couple of sizes.

Many people have the impression that chisels are always struck with a large wooden mallet. This used to be the case when chisels were made only with wooden handles which would have split if struck with a hammer.

Nowadays, chisels are made with unbreakable plastic handles so make sure that you get this type. This will avoid the expense of having to buy a mallet.

The chisel is potentially the most dangerous tool in the tool kit. If it gets blunt, or is used incorrectly, it could slip and cause a severely cut hand. So make sure you keep a sharp edge on a chisel (see page 40).

Take special care with chisels as the edges can be damaged easily. Do not throw them down on the table or drop them back into the toolbox after use.

Always keep both hands behind the cutting edge. You will be working with the chisel held either vertically or horizontally. The wood must be secured to a flat surface with a clamp, otherwise it will slip or splinter.

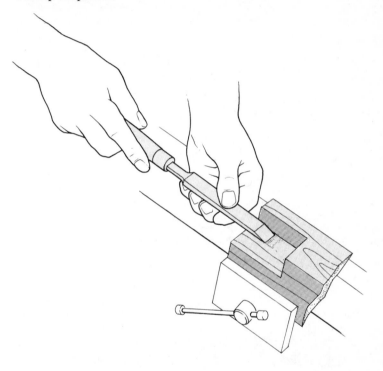

Always keep both hands behind the cutting edge of a chisel and see that the wood is securely held in a vice or clamped before commencing to work.

When paring wood (working with the grain), use a slicing action to take off a little at a time. With this type of operation, hand pressure alone is usually sufficient.

In vertical paring, place the thumb on top of the handle and curl the forefinger of the other hand across the blade to steady and guide it.

In horizontal paring, hold the handle in the palm of one hand with the forefinger pointing down the handle in the direction of the cut. Hold the blade with the other hand to ensure control and guidance. The little finger should curl round the blade near the cutting edge and the thumb should extend along the handle.

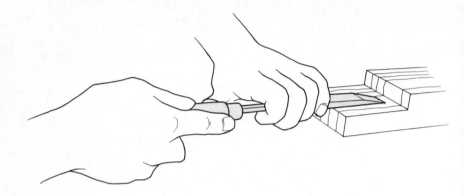

When paring horizontally, hold the handle in the palm of one hand with the forefinger pointing down the handle in the direction of the cut. The little finger should curl around the blade near the cutting edge and the thumb should extend along the handle. Waste piece of soft timber for chisel to go into.

When used with a mallet or hammer to chop out, say, a hinge slot, hold the chisel low down the handle. Use the hammer firmly but not severely. This method is used only when working across the grain since hand pressure alone will not be sufficient to remove any wood.

Rounding off corners is completed in easy stages. The main corners are cut off initially, then a series of smaller cuts is made until a round shape is achieved.

Avoid chopping downwards with the blade held right on the marked-out pencil line. If you do, the wedge shape of the edge will force the blade beyond the pencil line. Start about 3 mm ($\frac{1}{8}$ in) inside the line. The 3 mm ($\frac{1}{8}$ in) strip is the last to be removed and will curl away easily under slight taps from the hammer.

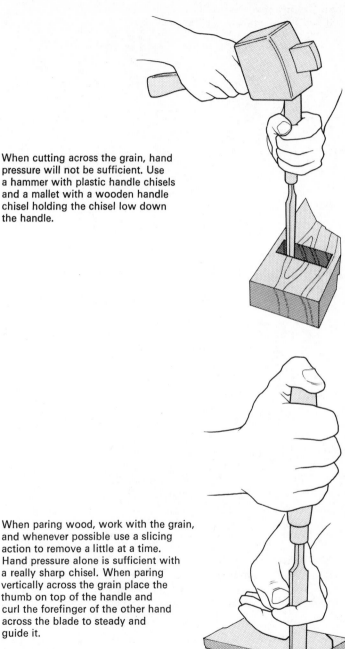

When cutting across the grain, hand
pressure will not be sufficient. Use
a hammer with plastic handle chisels
and a mallet with a wooden handle
chisel holding the chisel low down
the handle.

When paring wood, work with the grain,
and whenever possible use a slicing
action to remove a little at a time.
Hand pressure alone is sufficient with
a really sharp chisel. When paring
vertically across the grain place the
thumb on top of the handle and
curl the forefinger of the other hand
across the blade to steady and
guide it.

When chiselling to a straight line, always start cutting inside the marked line with the flat back of the blade towards the line. During the cutting operation the wedge shape front of the chisel will force the blade back to the line.

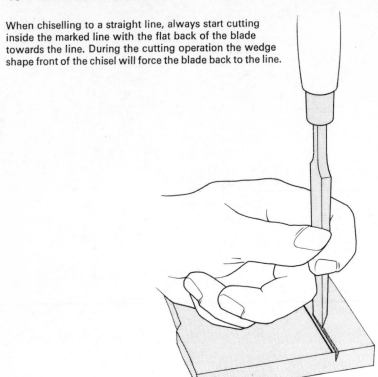

Sharpening chisel and plane blades

Chisels and plane iron blades must be kept sharp both for safety (blunt tools are likely to slip off the wood) and for easier working.

The blades of these tools must be at an angle of 25 degrees. The cutting edge must be at 30 degrees.

Sharpening accurately freehand takes a lot of experience so a honing guide (such as the Eclipse) is an invaluable acquisition for a beginner. This guide is used in conjunction with an oil stone. This is simply a piece of stone (usually carborundum), 8 ins × 2 ins × 1 in (200 mm × 50 mm × 25 mm). The screw on the side of the honing guide clamps the blade in position at the required angle.

Smear the stone with a little light oil such as the type used for bicycles or for softening leather (linseed oil is too thick for this purpose). Work the blade back and forth over the stone until you

can detect with your fingers a burr (roughness) on the back edge.
To remove this burr, lay that side of the blade flat on the stone and
rub it along the stone to 'polish off' the burr.

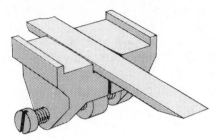

A honing guide will assist to sharpen chisel and plane iron blades
accurately when using an oil stone.

Hammering – hammer, nail punch and pincers

Several different types of hammers are made for various trades. As
far as the woodworker is concerned only two will be of interest.
These are the Warrington or pein hammer and the claw hammer.

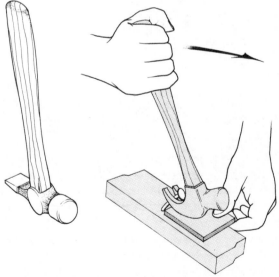

A medium-weight 10 oz (about 280 gm) claw hammer is used to drive
nails into timber as well as extracting them with the claw. A lighter-weight
6 oz (about 170 gm) Warrington hammer is useful for starting and driving
in small nails and pins.

The Warrington is solely for knocking in nails (although it is perfectly suitable for use with a chisel). The tapered side of the head is for getting into awkward corners and for starting to tap home small panel pins which have to be held between the fingers until they are partly driven into the workpiece. This is the hammer to buy for general woodwork.

The claw hammer is designed for heavier work involving large nails. The claw shape will extract nails which have been knocked home incorrectly.

Alternatively, pincers can be used to extract nails.

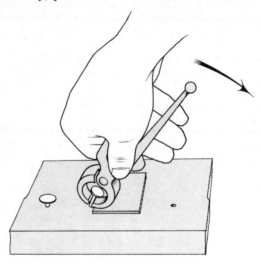

Pincers are useful as an alternative tool for extracting nails from timber. Use scrap wood to prevent the pincers or hammer claw from bruising the surface of the timber.

The heavier a hammer, the more easily it will knock home nails, especially long ones. However, since when you start woodwork you are not likely to be using nails in excess of 75 mm (3 ins) there is no point in buying a heavyweight hammer.

Buy a hammer of a weight to suit your physique. The extra force exerted by a heavier hammer will be wasted if you are unable to apply it correctly. A 10 oz (about 280 gm) hammer is a good, average weight that suits most people.

Unlike a saw, plane or chisel, which have to be kept sharp, little maintenance is needed with a hammer, though dirt or glue adhering to the striking surface could make the hammer slip off the nail head, giving you a bruised thumb. It is also the cause of nails being driven home incorrectly. Clean the faces of the hammer with glasspaper so that they will always grip the nail head.

Hold the hammer firmly, not tightly, at the end of the handle. Holding it halfway down results in loss of power – the full weight is not used. Firm control will enable you to use the hammer with an easy swing action which applies its full weight. A tight grip means the hammer is 'pushed' at the nail head and more often than not will bend the nail.

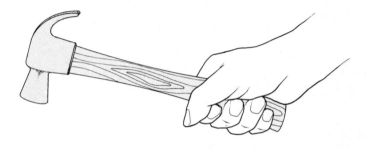

Hold the hammer towards the end of the handle for the most efficient use. Holding the hammer higher up the shaft will result in a considerable loss of power.

Keep your eye on the nail head and strike the head of the nail with the flat face of the hammer.

A nail or pin head is not an attractive sight, and these must be knocked below the surface so that a woodfiller can be used to fill the hole and obliterate them. To drive a nail head below surface, you will need a nail punch. This is a steel, pencil-like implement with a cupped pointed end which sits securely on the nail head.

Stop using the hammer when the nail head is just above the surface. If the hammer is allowed to strike the wood, it will leave a circular bruise on the surface.

Hold the punch carefully in position on the nail and tap the other end with sufficient pressure until the head sinks fractionally – about 1 mm ($\frac{1}{32}$ in) – below the surface.

Inevitably nails sometimes have to be withdrawn – even professionals make mistakes. To protect the surface from bruising, slip a small piece of wood under the jaws of the pincers. This will also

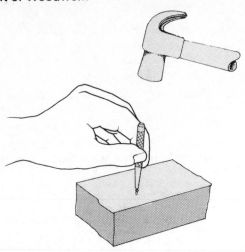

Use a hammer and steel nail punch to drive nails and pins below the surface of the timber. Remember that to try to drive a nail flush with the surface will result in badly bruising the timber.

increase the leverage on the jaws and make the nail come out more easily. The same principle applies when using a claw hammer to extract a nail.

Drilling holes

It is necessary to make holes for screws otherwise they split the wood as they sink in.

A detailed description of how to determine the correct length and thickness of a hole is given on page 58.

For making starter holes for small screws, cup hooks, screw eyes and so on, there is a choice of three tools – an awl, a bradawl or a gimlet. The first and last have a tendency to split the grain if a hole is started near the edge of a piece of wood.

This leaves the bradawl, the best all-purpose tool in the three. It has a flat chisel-like point.

Keep the cutting edge of the bradawl across the grain. If it is used parallel with the grain it will force the fibres apart and cause a split.

The bradawl is not turned in a full circle. An alternate clockwise/anti-clockwise wiggling action is used. You will soon develop the required amount of hand pressure to use to force the cutting edge into the wood. Obviously, the bradawl will make holes of only one diameter.

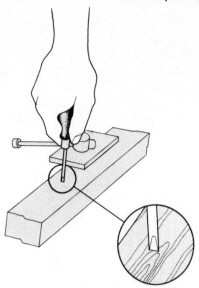

A starter hole for small screws can be made with an awl, bradawl or gimlet.

Use the small chisel point of a bradawl across the grain, to reduce the
risk of splitting the timber.

All larger holes are made with either an electric drill, a hand drill
or a brace. These basic units are fitted with attachments called twist
drills and auger bits, which actually drill the holes in the wood. They
are fitted quickly into the chuck (the nose part) of the basic unit
and will take a collection of these attachments in order to drill a
range of hole sizes.

Nowadays, the electric drill is almost as common in the home
as a vacuum cleaner. Apart from drilling holes in wood, walls and
so on, it can be fitted with a variety of accessories for such jobs
as hedge trimming or car polishing.

Since a drill must revolve at different speeds when going into
different materials, it is sensible to buy a two-speed drill at the outset.
A single-speed drill will be a little cheaper but has more limited
uses.

The lower of the two speeds is used when drilling into masonry,
and brickwork. The higher speed is for drilling into wood.

The electric drill is used with twist drills for wood work. If you
want to make holes in brickwork you must use a masonry drill with
a harder point made of tungsten carbide.

A hand drill simply drills holes in a variety of materials and is used with a twist drill or a masonry drill. Its advantage over an electric drill is its much lower price. The drill is operated by turning the handle at a constant speed, not too fast. Do not let the drill wobble otherwise the hole will be bigger than you intended and the twist drill could break off in the hole.

To withdraw the drill from the hole, keep turning the handle

Larger holes should be made using a twist drill of the appropriate size with either a hand drill or an electric drill.

in a clockwise direction and gradually pull it backwards. As the drill leaves the hole it will bring the waste wood shavings with it.

When drilling deep holes – say 25 mm (1 in) or more – the twist drill can become clogged with waste. Avoid this by withdrawing it frequently and clearing the shavings off.

If you are concerned exclusively with woodwork and intend to go on to bigger and better things you should buy a brace. This is used with auger bits which can be used only on wood.

There are two types of brace: an ordinary type and a ratchet type. The ordinary brace is operated by turning the handle in a full circle. The advantage of the ratchet brace is that the handle can operate also in a part circle. This is especially useful when drilling a

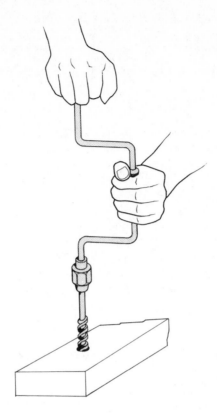

A hand brace is used with larger auger bits to drill larger holes for inserting small pipes, etc.

hole in a tight corner where it is impossible to turn the handle in a full circle. This is how it works.

The handle is turned as much as the corner allows: it is then reversed to the starting point. On the reverse sweep, the auger bit remains stationary. Another forward sweep drives the auger a little further into the wood, and so on. The ratchet brace is a little more expensive but well worth the extra outlay.

When drilling right through a piece of wood, bore the hole until the tip of the auger appears on the reverse side. This precaution is necessary otherwise the auger will split the wood as it emerges fully.

This method is not possible with a thin piece of wood since, as the tip of the auger appears on the reverse side, it will not have started to form the hole on the starting side. Overcome this problem by clamping a spare piece of wood to the thin piece being cut. Drilling right through into the spare piece will give you a clean hole in the thin piece.

Twist drills and auger bits

In theory, twist drills and auger bits correspond in diameter with all the various screw diameter sizes. Thus an $\frac{11}{16}$ in diameter drill or auger is supposed to drill an $\frac{11}{16}$ in diameter hole for an $\frac{11}{16}$ in diameter screw. It may do. Sometimes, though, you will find that the screw will not go into the drilled hole very easily, or it will go in too easily and not grip very well. Obviously, then, the hole is something less or more than $\frac{11}{16}$ in.

You can try putting a little soap on the thread of the screw. This will sometimes overcome any minor tightness. The only alternative, if that fails, is to select the next largest drill or bit and make the hole a little larger. If you make a note of this, you will not waste time when you next use the $\frac{11}{16}$ in drill.

There is no hard-and-fast rule about which drill or bit sizes you should buy initially. The best way is to get them as the need arises. One thing you will need is a countersunk bit. This fits into both a brace and a drill.

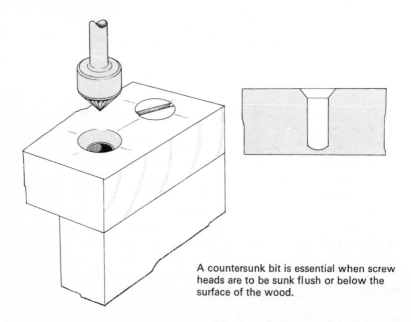

A countersunk bit is essential when screw heads are to be sunk flush or below the surface of the wood.

The first thing to master is drilling a hole in a true vertical at right angles to the surface so that the hole will come out exactly where you intended on the other side of the wood. The only guaranteed way to drill squarely is to use an electric drill in a drill stand.

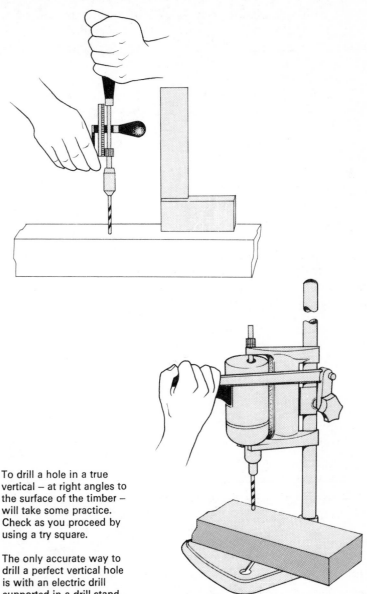

To drill a hole in a true vertical – at right angles to the surface of the timber – will take some practice. Check as you proceed by using a try square.

The only accurate way to drill a perfect vertical hole is with an electric drill supported in a drill stand.

However, reasonable accuracy can be achieved by using as a guide something that you know to be accurate – for example, a try square.

It is difficult to judge whether the drill is leaning towards or away from you. With practice, however, you will develop a feel for this. In the meantime, do not worry, just do your best. Any inaccuracy is bound to be marginal and should not spoil the job.

Drilling square into a wall must be left to the judgement of the eye. However, extreme accuracy is not usually necessary so any minor mistakes should not matter.

Sometimes a twist drill will wander off its intended position as it first tries to bite into the wood. Overcome this by making a small starter hole with a bradawl or lightly tap a small nail point in the exact drilling position. The drill will then grip the starter hole and will not jump about.

When drilling into a wall, use a nail to make a starter hole for the masonry drill.

Auger bits used with a brace have their own built-in starter hole thread and will not wander about.

Often it is necessary to drill a hole to the required depth into the timber – rather than straight through it. Drilling a hole to the correct depth for a screw is normally done with a gadget called a depth stop. This fits on to the twist drill or auger bit only allowing the desired portion to enter the wood.

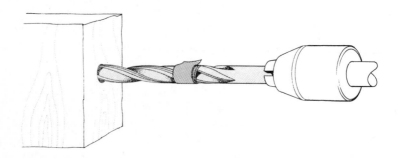

Wrap a piece of coloured adhesive tape around the shaft of a twist drill to determine the exact depth of the hole to be drilled.

A simple method, however, is to wrap a piece of adhesive tape to the twist drill or auger bit in the required position. When it reaches the surface, stop drilling.

Screwdrivers

Screwdrivers are made in a variety of sizes and blade widths. Generally speaking the longer the blade, the wider the tip that engages the screw slot. This is no hard and fast rule however. The essential requirement is to have a selection of blade tip widths in your kit.

The range of sizes is necessary since the tip of the blade must be a good fit in the screw slot – and there are many sizes of screw available.

Always use a screwdriver that fits comfortably into the screw slot. If it is too small, the screwdriver will not be able to turn the screw and the tip will damage the sides of the slot. If it is too wide it will project beyond the slot and score the wood on the final few turns.

For basic purposes, you should keep three sizes of screwdriver in your toolbox – 75 mm (3 ins), 150 mm (6 ins) and 200 mm (8 ins). These will deal adequately with the most generally used screw sizes.

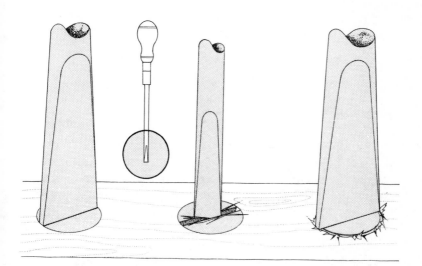

Always use a screwdriver, the blade of which fits accurately into the screw slot.

If too small the screwdriver blade will not be able to turn the screw and will damage the head, often resulting in razor sharp slivers of steel or brass which will splinter and cut the fingers.

If the screwdriver is too wide for the head of the screw, the blade will project beyond the slot and damage the wood on the final few turns.

The measurements refer to the length of the blade and do not include the handle.

Driving home a lot of screws can be hard work. Now, though, there are ratchet screwdrivers and spiral ratchet screwdrivers which make life a lot easier.

Ratchet screwdrivers work like a ratchet brace. The handle is turned clockwise to drive the screw in. Each turn is completed, the handle returns to the starting point leaving the screw stationary. Thus a screw can be driven home without disengaging the tip of the screwdriver from the slot.

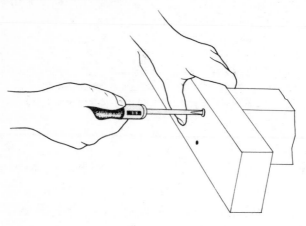

A ratchet screwdriver works like a ratchet hand brace and is a useful tool when driving or unscrewing a lot of screws, as the hand does not have to be released from the handle during the operation.

A spiral ratchet screwdriver, though more expensive again, is the best buy of all. A decent size model is supplied with a selection of interchangeable blades which are fitted, as required, into the chuck. Thus it is really several screwdrivers in one.

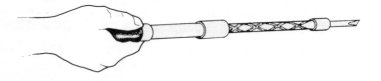

The Yankee spiral screwdriver has all the advantages of the ratchet screwdriver and also works more quickly because of its pump action. Several interchangeable blades can be used to cover most screw requirements

It is operated like a bicycle pump. Instead of turning, you push the handle. A spiral action translates the pushes into a turning movement of the blade. A built-in spring returns the barrel to the starting point. If used correctly, these screwdrivers are a reliable investment.

The tip of a screwdriver must be kept square always. If, through misuse, it becomes rounded off, it will slip out of the slot and may damage the screwhead or the surface of the wood.

A worn or damaged blade should be reground (at a tool merchant's shop) to form a clean, square edge. Always keep the tip of the screwdriver tightly located in the slot with firm hand pressure. The hand not holding the handle should be used to steady the blade and ensure it stays in place.

G cramps

The G cramp gets its name from its shape. When two pieces of wood are joined, the G cramp can be used to hold them together until the

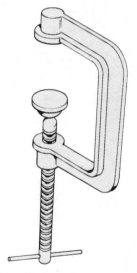

The G cramp is ideal either for securing a workpiece to the bench to keep both hands free for working or for holding pieces of timber together while adhesive is setting.
Note: The pressure of a cramp when tightened will bruise the surface of finished timber so protect the surface with scrap slivers of wood under the jaws.

The size of the cramp is governed by the size of the jaw opening when fully unscrewed. An 200 mm (8 in) cramp is a useful general purpose size, but a range of sizes are worth purchasing.

adhesive between them has set. Another important use is for securing a workpiece to the table top thus leaving both hands free for work.

G cramps come in a range of sizes from 50 mm to 300 mm (2 ins to 12 ins). This dimension denotes the width of the jaw opening. 200 mm (8 ins) is a useful size as it will grip tightly any two pieces of wood that you are likely to be fixing together and will also secure a single piece tightly to a table top. Anyone who progresses with woodwork in a serious way will find that a whole set of these inexpensive little gadgets is invaluable.

When a cramp is tightened on a workpiece, the jaws can bruise the surface. Prevent this by placing small pieces of wood between the jaws and the workpiece.

A worksurface

Keen woodworkers will probably have purpose-made workbenches permanently installed in the garage or in a shed in the garden.

The beginner, however, usually works on the kitchen table. No matter how careful you are, you will eventually scratch the

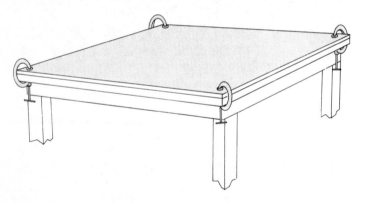

A good working surface can be provided by clamping down a sheet of 12 mm ($\frac{1}{2}$ in) plywood onto a solid table using small G clamps at each corner.

table top, so make a temporary worksurface by covering the table with a sheet of 12 mm ($\frac{1}{2}$ in) thick plywood, secured at each corner with a G cramp.

4. Joining and Fixing

To make a piece of furniture, be it a shelf or a fitted wardrobe, all the pieces of wood have to be sawn and planed to size and then joined together.

The simplest method of joining is to use a butt joint. This section describes three different types of butt joint: screws, nails, and the slightly more sophisticated and stronger butt joint made from small pieces of wood called dowels (see page 62). Screws or nails alone are not sufficient to hold together a joint in a piece of furniture that has to withstand normal wear and tear. The use of glue gives the joint the essential extra strength. Take a coffee table, for example.

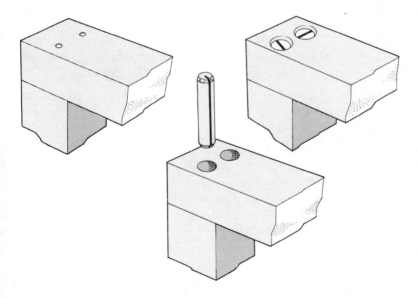

The simplest way to make a joint between two pieces of wood is to make a butt joint, using glue and nails or screws.

Alternatively dowels can be used. To be really successful these must be accurately aligned and a dowelling jig will be necessary to achieve this.

Even in the most careful household it has to withstand a good deal of punishment: it is moved about the room, bumped with the vacuum cleaner, sat upon by the children or knocked by their toys. All this puts pressure on the weakest parts, the joints, so these have to be strong.

Butt joint with screws

The advantage of a screw over a nail is that it has greater holding power and can be removed easily. It makes a joint considerably stronger and should be used on any piece of furniture that will have to withstand a reasonable amount of strain.

Screws come in all shapes and sizes. For basic purposes, however, the choice can be narrowed down considerably. The three things to consider are the shape of the head, the length and the thickness.

There are two head shapes in common use in woodwork – a countersunk head and a raised countersunk head.

The countersunk head is the one you will usually use as most jobs require the screw head to be sunk level with, or slightly below the surface. The countersunk screw is designed to sink either flush with the surface or a fraction below it so that it can be obliterated by covering it with a woodfiller.

The head of the raised countersunk screw finishes partly above and partly below the surface. This is used purely for decorative appearances, if so desired. Often it is used with screw cups for a neater finish.

Raised countersunk screws are often used with screw cups for a decorative finish to a joint.

When fixing door hinges, only the countersunk can be used. This is because the two leaves of the hinge must close tightly together. The raised countersunk would prevent this.

The modern screws, Philips and Pozidriv can be used if you prefer the appearance of their star-shaped slots. It is essential to use the correct screwdriver (special types named after the screw) otherwise the screwhead will be damaged easily.

Screw lengths increase in increments of 6 mm ($\frac{1}{4}$ in). In basic work, your needs will fall within the 6 mm ($\frac{1}{4}$ in) to 75 mm (3 in) range.

An easy guide to the length needed is that the screw should be three times the thickness of the top piece of wood. Thus, if fixing a 12 mm ($\frac{1}{2}$ in) thick piece of wood to a piece of wood of any other thickness, the screw length will need to be three times 12 mm— 36 mm ($\frac{1}{2}$ in—$1\frac{1}{2}$ ins).

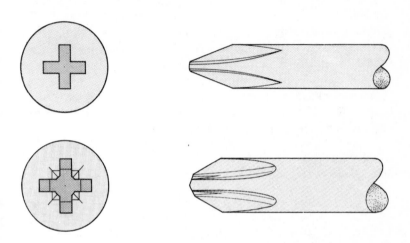

It is essential to use the correct screwdriver when using a Philips screw, likewise the correct Pozidriv screwdriver should be used with the Pozidriv screw.

Finally, there is the thickness of the screw. The thickness is the diameter of the shank. This dimension is called the gauge and is expressed as a number.

The smallest gauge (number 1) is 1·78 mm ($\frac{1}{16}$ in). The largest gauge (number 14) is 6·30 mm ($\frac{11}{16}$ in).

For basic work, you need only concern yourself with three sizes: number 8 4·17 mm ($\frac{11}{64}$ in) is by far the most commonly used, but you will have occasional use for the slightly smaller number 6 3·45 mm ($\frac{9}{64}$ in) and the slightly larger number 10 4·88 mm ($\frac{3}{16}$ in).

Thus a screw which is 50 mm (2 ins) long, 4·17 mm ($\frac{11}{64}$ in) in diameter and has a countersunk head, is referred to as a 50 mm (2 ins) number 8 countersunk screw.

Do not be alarmed by all this. It boils down to the fact that normally you will be using a number 8 countersunk screw. The only thing you have to determine for yourself is the correct length.

Fixing two pieces of wood together involves drilling two holes. The hole in the top piece (called the clearance hole) goes right through the wood to accommodate the head and the shank of the screw. The hole in the lower piece (called the pilot hole) accommodates the threaded part of the screw.

The threaded part holds the lower piece to the top piece. Thus the hole made for it must not be too large or the thread will not grip on to the wood. Nor, however, must it be too tight otherwise the screw may split the wood as it goes in. The hole in the top piece should be slightly bigger than the shank since the shank must go in easily and does not do any holding.

Below is a table which gives the correct size holes to make for the commonly used screws. As you can see, the pilot hole is roughly half the diameter of the clearance hole.

Screw gauge No	Diameter of screw		Clearance hole diameter		Pilot hole diameter	
	mm	in.	mm	in.	mm	in.
4	2·74	$\frac{7}{64}$	2·75	$\frac{1}{8}$	1·70	$\frac{5}{64}$
6	3·45	$\frac{9}{64}$	3·40	$\frac{5}{32}$	2·10	$\frac{5}{64}$
8	4·17	$\frac{11}{64}$	4·20	$\frac{3}{16}$	2·50	$\frac{3}{32}$
10	4·88	$\frac{3}{16}$	4·90	$\frac{7}{32}$	2·75	$\frac{1}{8}$
12	5·59	$\frac{7}{32}$	5·60	$\frac{1}{4}$	3·15	$\frac{1}{8}$

The correct procedure for drilling the two holes is as follows:

1   Drill a hole in the top piece (clearance hole) that will enable the shank of the screw to turn easily.

2   Drill a countersunk hole for the screw head so that when the screw is fully home, the head will be a fraction below surface.

3   Position the two pieces of wood in their intended places and use a bradawl to mark the centre of the hole in the lower piece (pilot hole).

4   Bore the pilot hole. Use a piece of tape tied to the drill to indicate the correct depth the drill should reach. This should be slightly less than the length of the thread.

5   Replace the top piece of wood in position and insert the screw.

A special set of drill bits for use with hand or power equipment

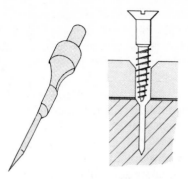

A range of special 'Screwmate' bits are available which will cut pilot, shaft and countersink holes in one operation, for screwing two pieces of wood together.

is available. These make pilot holes, shank clearance and counter-sunks to the correct depths all in one operation. Called the Stanley Screw Mate, they are available in a range of sizes.

Butt joint with nails and glue

A reasonably strong joint can be made with nails and glue but it will not have the strength of a screwed and glued joint. This method should not be used where a joint will have to withstand a lot of wear and tear.

Nails do have the advantage over screws that they are simpler and quicker to use. Three types are commonly used: the oval wire nail, the round wire nail and the panel pin.

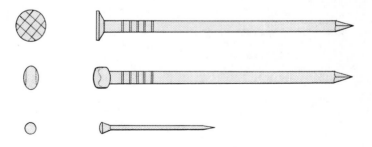

Round wire nail (French nail). Oval wire nail. Panel pin.

Where appearance is important, use an oval wire nail. Its head can be punched below surface with a nail punch and covered with woodfiller. It is used to fix wood which is 12 mm ($\frac{1}{2}$ in) thick or more. Common size range is 20 mm ($\frac{3}{4}$ in) to 150 mm (6 ins long).

The round wire nail has a large head that remains on the surface and is therefore no use if appearance is important. It is used mainly in outdoor or temporary structures. Common range size is 20 mm ($\frac{3}{4}$ in) to 150 mm (6 ins) long.

The panel pin is a small, thin nail with a head that can be punched below surface and covered with woodfiller. It is needed for finer work such as fixing mouldings, hardboard or thinner plywoods, or for making picture frames. Common size range is 15 mm ($\frac{5}{8}$ in) to 75 mm (3 ins) long.

Generally speaking, a nail should be three to four times longer than the thickness of the top piece of wood being fixed.

A common problem with nails is that they split the grain as they sink in. Prime causes of this are using too thick a nail, nailing too near the edge of a piece of wood and putting two or more nails in a straight line along the grain.

An oval wire nail is less likely than a round wire nail to split the wood if it is inserted with its flat sides parallel with the grain. However, this is no guarantee. There are extra precautions you can take.

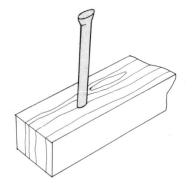

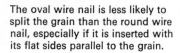
The oval wire nail is less likely to split the grain than the round wire nail, especially if it is inserted with its flat sides parallel to the grain.

First, blunt the point of the nail by nipping it off with pincers. It is the sharp point which causes splitting by tearing the fibres of the wood apart.

Second, drill a starter hole for the nail. Use a bradawl for smaller nails. Use a twist drill which is about four-fifths the diameter of larger nails.

Third, stagger the positions of the nails if two or more have to be used for fixing.

A nailed joint can be made stronger by knocking the nails in either sloping towards or away from each other. If they are knocked in straight, they are more likely to be pushed straight out again if brought under strain.

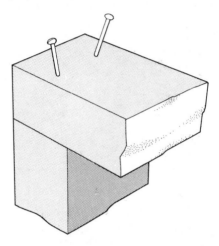

A nailed joint will be made stronger by knocking the nails through the timber at an angle, either towards or away from each other.

Butt joint with dowelling

Butt-jointing two pieces of wood together using dowels and glue provides an even stronger joint than nails or screws.

Corresponding holes are drilled in the two pieces of wood being joined. The dowels are located in the holes and the two pieces of wood joined together over them.

Two dowels are needed in each butt joint to prevent the possibility of the wood twisting out of place later.

Dowels are cut from hardwood dowelling rod – stocked by all timber merchants in various diameters from $\frac{1}{16}$ in (2 mm) to 1 in (25 mm) and usually sold in 7 ft (about 2100 mm) lengths.

The right size diameter dowel is determined by the wood being joined. The dowels must be about one third the thickness of the wood. So, if you are using 25 mm (1 in) thick wood, you will need

$\frac{3}{8}$ in (10 mm) diameter dowel. Using 50 mm (2 ins) thick wood, you will need $\frac{3}{4}$ in (20 mm) diameter dowel, and so on.

The difficult part of the job is to drill the holes correctly. Since dowels will not bend, the holes must be exactly opposite each other – and be truly vertical.

The positions of the holes can be ascertained by accurate measuring and marking or you can buy a special gadget called a dowelling

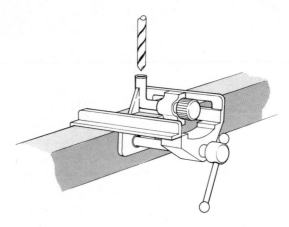

Alternatively dowels can be used. To be really successful these must be accurately aligned and a dowelling jig will be necessary to achieve this.

jig which enables dowel holes to be bored with perfect accuracy every time. It certainly reduces the time spent on precision marking.

A simple jig can be made from a piece of plywood once you have succeeded in making an accurate dowel joint. Obviously, though, this jig will be of value only when you are joining pieces of wood of similar widths to those used to make the jig. But, in time, you can build up a whole collection to suit different timber and dowel sizes, though by this time you might decide to buy a proper jig anyway.

A dowel must be about four times the length of its diameter. So, a $\frac{3}{8}$ in (10 mm) diameter dowel will be $1\frac{1}{2}$ ins (38 mm) long; a $\frac{3}{4}$ in (20 mm) dowel will be 3 ins (75 mm) long, and so on.

Half the dowel must sink into one piece of wood and half into the other piece. The hole must be drilled vertically and at exactly the right length in each piece of wood. If one hole is deeper than the other the joint will be weak; too short holes will prevent the wood joining up over the dowels.

The diameter of the hole is critical too. The dowel must be a snug fit in the hole, not too tight, not too loose.

Dowelling rod, like wood, is sold in a nominal thickness. Thus a $\frac{3}{8}$ in (10 mm) diameter dowel may be slightly less than its stated size. A $\frac{3}{8}$ in drill or bit may make too big a hole for the dowel. You may need to use a drill or bit which is $\frac{1}{16}$ in smaller. Here, for example, you would select a $\frac{5}{16}$ in diameter drill or bit. So practise first on a scrap piece of wood.

The holes, therefore, must be drilled accurately to thickness.

Chamfer (bevel) the ends of each dowel, as shown, using a sharp

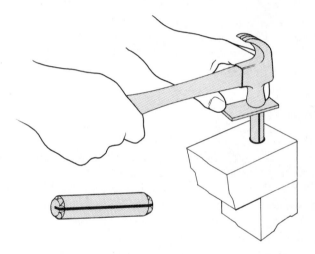

When using dowels, slightly chamfer the ends before glueing into position. This will help to prevent the dowel splitting the wood. Always cut a shallow groove along the length of each dowel to allow the pressure of glue to escape when the joint is formed. Tap a dowel into position using a block of wood to prevent the hammer from damaging the end of the dowel.

knife. This is a worthwhile precaution to prevent any possibility of the wood splitting as the dowel is tapped in.

Use a hammer and a spare piece of wood to tap both dowels into the holes and join up the two pieces of wood over them. If the hammer is used directly on to the dowel, the end will burr over or split away and prevent easy access into the remaining hole.

It often happens that when the glue has been smeared on the dowels, the joint will not close up. If you make a saw cut along the length of each dowel, excess glue will be allowed to escape along the channel and the two pieces of wood will be able to join up.

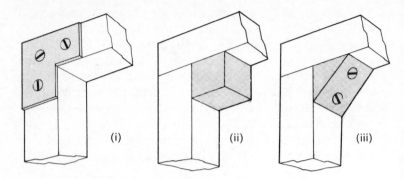

(i)   (ii)   (iii)

Butt joints can be strengthened in various ways.
 (i) By screwing a metal corner plate to the outer edge of the joint.
 (ii) By screwing a 25 mm (1 in) square piece of wood along the inside
      edge.
(iii) By screwing a triangular section of wood along the inside edge.

Strengthening a butt joint

Eventually, you will have the confidence to make a larger unit, say
a wardrobe. This needs stronger joints than a small table because
when it is moved around for cleaning, decorating or whatever, then
all the weight will be taken by the joints. Normally, more sophisticated joints are used here by cutting certain shapes out of one piece
of wood to marry up with other shapes cut from a second piece.
Since no external agent (nails, screws or dowels) has been used,
wood is gripping on to wood giving a much stronger construction.

   Beginners can strengthen a butt joint, however it was made, by
one of three methods:

   By screwing on a metal corner plate or L-shaped plate. These
are sold in d-i-y shops.

   By screwing a 25 mm (1 in) square strip of wood along the complete inside edge.

   Slightly more difficult, by cutting a triangular block and screwing
this into place. This involves drilling holes at an angle, but should
not present problems since only reasonable accuracy is sufficient.

Knock Down (KD) fittings

Anyone who finds that they cannot make a proper joint with the
three methods described has an alternative in KD (knock down)
fittings.

The term knock down is used in the furniture industry to describe any unit of furniture which is delivered to the customer in kit form ready for home assembly. The units are said to be 'knocked down' into a kit of parts. Kitchen units are the most popular form.

KD fittings are often included to make the job of assembly easier for the customer. These plastic fittings can, however, be bought individually from d-i-y shops.

To make a butt joint you need the one shown below, a Handi-joint. This comes in two parts. The parts are screwed separately to the two pieces of wood being joined and are then bolted together so that a perfect butt joint is formed. Screws are supplied with the fitting.

The obvious disadvantage of these fittings is their cost. Individually they are not expensive but since one has to be used at each corner of a unit, the cost mounts up considerably.

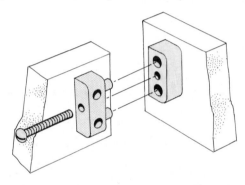

Butt joints can easily by constructed by using KD joints such as the plastic Handi-joint. These joints are ideal when making furniture which has to be dismantled periodically.

Adhesives

Although there is a wide range of adhesives available, for your initial purposes, you can confine yourself to two types: PVA adhesives and impact adhesives.

PVA adhesives are sold ready to use from a tube or a tin. Read the manufacturer's instructions before using them.

Generally speaking, they are spread evenly on both surfaces and the two are brought together while the adhesive is still wet. This allows time for any adjustments to be made to the position of the wood before G cramps are applied.

Brand names to look out for include: Bostik Carpentry, Dufix and Evo-Stik Resin W.

Impact adhesives are used straight from the tube or tin – again, follow manufacturer's instructions.

Generally they are spread evenly on both surfaces and left until touch dry before the surfaces are brought together and tapped firmly to ensure a good join. The bond on impact is really strong.

The obvious advantage with impact types is that work can proceed immediately without having to apply G cramps and waiting for the glue to set. However, they are best avoided initially by the beginner who might not get the positioning of the two pieces of wood right first time though after a while you will feel confident about using them.

Brand names to look out for include: Evo-Stik Impact, Clam 3, Bostik 3 and Dunlop Thixofix.

Making use of a butt joint

Basically, any simple piece of furniture is a box, be it a shelf unit, a storage chest or a large wardrobe. You can make any of these using only butt joints.

The materials to use depend on three factors – your ability, the size of the unit, and the cost of materials. If you can make a successful butt joint then you can minimize the cost.

If the unit is less than 150 mm (6 ins) wide, natural wood can be used to make the complete unit. Or you can, if you prefer, use man-made boards. The cost difference will not be great.

However, when you need panels wider than 150 mm (6 ins) you have two choices. The cheapest method is to make a framework using 50 mm × 25 mm (2 ins × 1 in) softwood (or 25 mm × 25 mm (1 in × 1 in) if the unit is to be small – (a display case for lightweight ornaments, for example) and then to cover it with 3 mm ($\frac{1}{8}$ in) or 6 mm ($\frac{1}{4}$ in) thick hardboard or plywood.

The alternative is to use complete panels of man-made boards such as chipboard, plywood or blockboard which is at least $\frac{1}{2}$ in thick. Here, the cost of making the unit will be increased considerably, though the time spent in doing the work will be reduced appreciably. The unit will also be a lot heavier. The increased weight could be important if you have to move it about for cleaning the floor underneath.

Below is a typical framework in 50 mm × 25 mm (2 ins × 1 in) softwood made using butt joints.

The two side frames are made first. Four rails are then cut to join together the two side frames. The framework will become stable when the 3 mm ($\frac{1}{8}$ in) or 6 mm ($\frac{1}{4}$ in) hardboard or plywood has been fixed.

Five panels are needed: one to cover each side, and one each for the back, the top and the bottom. Use panel pins at every 100 mm (4 ins) to secure the panels to the softwood.

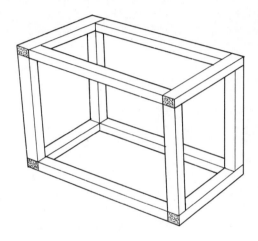

Cutting those panels to the exact size is not easy. The beginner can easily make a sawing error leaving a panel a little bit too small.

The easiest way to overcome this problem is to cut and fix the panels about 2 mm ($\frac{1}{16}$ in) oversize all round. When time has been allowed for the glue to set, use a plane or a Surform to trim the protruding edges flush with the softwood framework. Finish planing one panel to size before fixing on the next. This way all edges will be accessible.

Shelves

If you want a shelf in the unit, you will have to fix a length of softwood in each side frame at the required position for the shelf. This must be done when the two side frames are made up otherwise you will have a terrible time trying to work inside the finished unit. These extra softwood lengths are called bearers since they bear the weight of the shelf.

It is best to use a reasonably thick – at least 12 mm ($\frac{1}{2}$ in) – soft-wood or man-made board for a shelf. You may only intend to keep light objects on it, but in future, something heavier may have to be stored.

Fix the shelf to the bearers before fitting the hardboard or plywood panels to the framework. This will make it easier to drill the holes through the four corners of the shelf into the bearers; it will be easier also to drive home the fixing screws.

Always use screws in this situation. Hammering in pins or nails will put a lot of strain on the framework. There is no need to use glue as well as screws for securing the shelf. Pressure will only be exerted downwards on the shelf from the items stored on it. There will be nothing pushing upwards from below. The screws just prevent the shelf from moving.

KD fittings (such as Handi-joints) can be used as shelf supports – one under each corner of the shelf. Screw these in place and fix the shelf before securing the side panels.

Alternative KD fittings to use are Handi-bearers. These would work out a little cheaper. A Handi-bearer consists of a threaded collar that is pushed into a pre-drilled hole (usually of the same diameter, but check manufacturer's instructions for exact details). Small bearers then slot into the collars and the shelf simply rests on top of them.

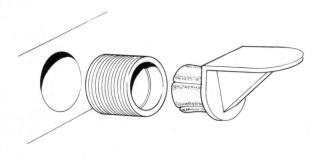

Fixing things to walls

Putting up shelves is something that almost everyone has to tackle at some time or other. It sounds simple enough – and it is if you know what you are doing. Tales of woe about shelves collapsing are usually the result of two things: either something is wrong with the screws or the shelf was overloaded.

A screw must be long enough and thick enough to be firmly fixed to the wall. The plaster that covers a brick wall is usually about 19 mm ($\frac{3}{4}$ in) thick. It is not strong enough to support a screw. The screw must penetrate through the plaster so that the threaded part is buried in the brickwork. The threaded part of the screw will not grip on to the brick, or for that matter on to any kind of masonry. The hole.drilled in the wall to receive the screw must be plugged first.

Wallplugs

A wallplug is a small hollow tube, made from either a fibrous material or plastic, which is pushed into the hole. The screw is then inserted into the plug. As the thread of the screw pushes in, it expands the walls of the plug which then grip on to the surrounding brickwork. Thus, when the screw is fully home, it is very tight indeed.

The hole drilled in the wall must be the exact length and thickness of the plug. The screw must be the exact length and diameter of the plug. To achieve this, you would therefore use a number 8 drill, a number 8 plug and a number 8 screw. Number 8 you will remember, means 4·17 mm ($\frac{11}{64}$ in) diameter.

To simplify things a little, some manufacturers (Rawlplug, for example) have introduced a system by which two plug sizes and two drill sizes can be used with any size screw between a number 6 and a number 12.

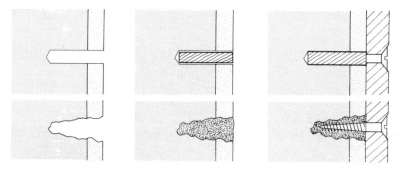

For a secure fixing a screw must penetrate the plaster and be buried well into the brickwork. A wallplug in plastic or fibre will be necessary to enable this as screws will not grip directly into brick or concrete.

An alternative to a wallplug is an asbestos fibre compound mixed with water and packed tightly into the screw hole. A screw can then be inserted directly into the compound.

An alternative to a wallplug is asbestos fibre filling compound. Brand names to look for include: Philplug, Screwfix and Rawlplug Compound.

This powdery material is supplied in small tins or cartons. It is especially useful where an oversize hole has been drilled in the wall. A sufficient amount of the powder is moistened with water to form a putty-like material and is rammed into the hole with the blunt end of the metal implement supplied in the tin. When the cavity is filled, the pointed end of the implement is used to make a starter hole for the screw in the centre of the compound. The screw can be driven home immediately and makes a very tight fixing.

Hollow walls

Walls vary in structure. Hollow partition walls (plasterboard over a wood framework, called studding) present a problem since the plaster is only 9 mm ($\frac{3}{8}$ in) thick, there are no bricks behind it, and it will not take a screw. A standard wallplug would simply drop into the cavity behind the plasterboard.

To meet this situation you can do one of two things.

One solution is that you can locate the wooden uprights of the framework and drive the screws into these. This has a couple of drawbacks. The position of the uprights can be located only by

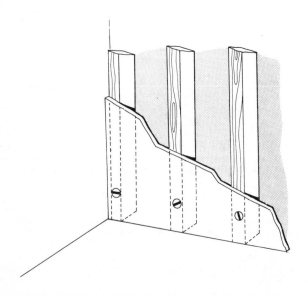

tapping along the plasterboard until the hollow sound becomes a dull thud which indicates something solid behind the surface – that is, an upright. This is not as easy as it sounds for an untrained ear. Besides, even when you find one upright, you still have to find at least one other to take a second fixing if, for example, you are putting up a shelf.

The neighbouring uprights are usually spaced at 400 mm (16 in), intervals which make them easier to locate. The trouble is, though, an upright might not fall in the position that you want to fix a screw at.

A better solution to the hollow-wall problem is to buy one of the special range of devices enabling you to fix a screw to the plaster-board itself.

There are three useful types that all work on the same principle, and all are available at d-i-y shops.

Gravity toggles   These have a hinged end section which is fed through the hole drilled in the plasterboard. Once behind, the hinged section drops down at right angles. As the screw is tightened, the hinged section compresses against the back of the plasterboard acting as an anchor. These devices cannot be removed intact from the wall.

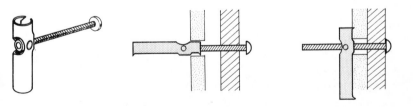

Rawlanchors   These have thin metal arms which spread out behind the plaster board as the screw is tightened at the front. A rawlanchor has one advantage; it stays in place when the screw is removed.

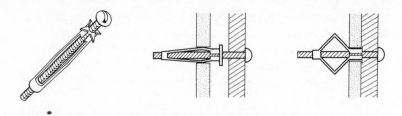

Spring toggles These have wings which fly open after they are passed through the hole made in the plasterboard. As the screw is tightened at the front, the wings grip securely to the back of the plasterboard. Once the screw is in, it cannot be removed without breaking the device.

  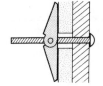

Putting up a shelf

A shelf must rest on something. You can buy brackets which are screwed to the wall over wood supports. This is the easiest but most expensive method.

The cheapest way is to fix lengths of softwood to the wall to act as bearers. The thickness of the softwood bearers and the size and the number of the screws used to fix them depends entirely on the load that the shelf is going to take.

The load that a shelf will take is impossible to express in exact figures. It is largely a matter of commonsense. All that can be given is a general yardstick.

For example, if a kitchen shelf is going to be used for storing saucepans and similar heavy objects, then you would use 50 mm × 25 mm (2 ins × 1 in) softwood bearers fixed with 65 mm (2½ ins) or 75 mm (3 ins) long, number 8 or number 10 screws.

On the other hand, for a small shelf to take lightweight ornaments, 25 mm × 25 mm (1 in × 1 in) softwood bearers fixed with 50 mm (2 ins) number 6 or number 8 screws will be adequate.

Intervals between screws in both cases should be no more than 300 mm (12 ins).

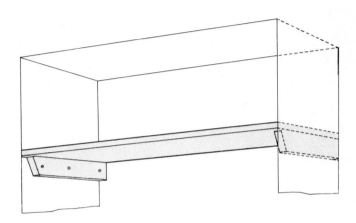

A recess or alcove is the most convenient position for a shelf. This is because the two end walls can be used for fixing the bearers. For spans longer than 915 mm (3 ft), you need a bearer screwed to the back wall as well, depending on the material used for the actual shelf. See table on page 74.

The problem with side wall bearers is that the end grain will show up under the shelf. End grain is not an attractive sight. So cut the bearers to leave them 50 mm (2 ins) short of the front edge of the shelf. This way they will not be seen.

A shelf is usually reasonably wide and over 915 mm (3 ft) long, so intermediate support between the end bearers or the brackets may have to be provided. If a bearer is screwed to the back wall, the distances below can be increased by a quarter. Thus 2440 mm (8 ft) without a back bearer can be 3050 mm (10 ft) with a back bearer.

The most economical material to use for a shelf is man-made boards. The thickness depends on the load the board is expected to take.

In the two examples given earlier, the kitchen shelf for saucepans should be 18 mm ($\frac{3}{4}$ in) or 25 mm (1 in) thick board; the shelf for light ornaments need be only 12 mm ($\frac{1}{2}$ in) thick.

Material	Thickness in mm (inches in brackets)	Maximum shelf span without intermediate support in mm (feet in brackets)
Chipboard	12($\frac{1}{2}$)	710(2)
	18($\frac{3}{4}$)	915 (3)
Blockboard and	12($\frac{1}{2}$)	1068(3·5)
plywood	18($\frac{3}{4}$)	1830(6)
	25(1)	2440(8)

5. Finishing Materials

This section is concerned purely with the various covering and finishing materials and the techniques for applying them.

Plastic laminate

This is available in large sheets, normally 2 mm ($\frac{1}{16}$ in) thick of varied pattern and colour. The surface is hardwearing and will resist normal stains like tea, cosmetics, ink and alcohol. It will not be damaged by a hot teapot but a frying pan or an electric iron straight from the heat will scorch it and may lift it away from the surface beneath.

It is easily cut with a Stanley trimming knife fitted with a laminated cutting blade – the normal blade is not suitable.

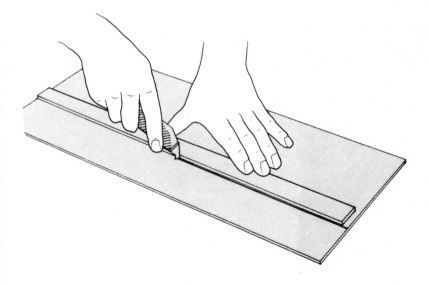

The most effective way to cut laminated plastic is to use either a Stanley knife fitted with a special laminate cutting blade or the more expensive Cintride laminate cutter.

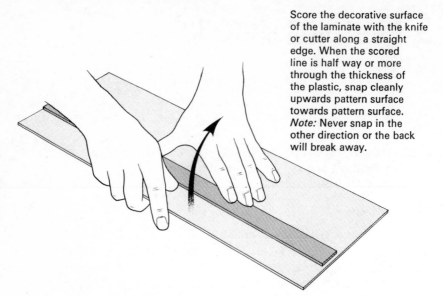

Score the decorative surface of the laminate with the knife or cutter along a straight edge. When the scored line is half way or more through the thickness of the plastic, snap cleanly upwards pattern surface towards pattern surface. *Note:* Never snap in the other direction or the back will break away.

Use a soft pencil to mark out cutting lines on the surface – these can be washed off later. Lay the sheet of laminate on a flat base with its decorative face uppermost. Hold the knife against a straight-edge. Score along the pencil line several times until either the laminate is cut right through or stop when it is halfway through and, holding the straight-edge firmly down, fold the waste side laminate upwards. It will break cleanly along the scored line.

A fine tooth handsaw, used at a low angle, will also cut the laminate. Saw through the sheet with the decorative face uppermost.

A fine toothed veneer saw can also be used to cut laminate from the decorative face side. The saw should be held at a shallow angle and the waste side supported to prevent tearing.

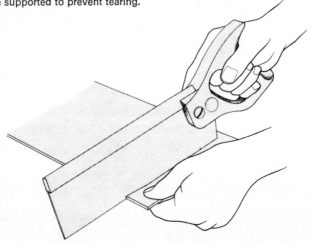

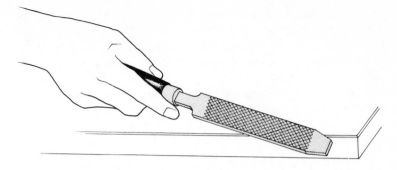

To trim off surplus laminate once it is firmly stuck in place use either a sharp block plane or a laminate trimming file.

Always cut the laminate about 3 mm ($\frac{1}{8}$ in) oversize. The surplus can be trimmed off when the laminate has been glued firmly in place.

To trim off, use a sharp block plane, or a special laminate trimming file. Trim off working away from the face of the laminate. Finish off by smoothing the edges with fine glasspaper or a sharp scraper.

Laminate is fixed with adhesive. Ideally use an impact adhesive which allows the edges to be trimmed immediately, but be careful to position the sheet accurately first time.

Use a row of drawing pins along the back edge of the surface to be covered so that the laminate can be positioned accurately if impact adhesive is to be used. This method can only be used if edging strips are to be stuck down last.

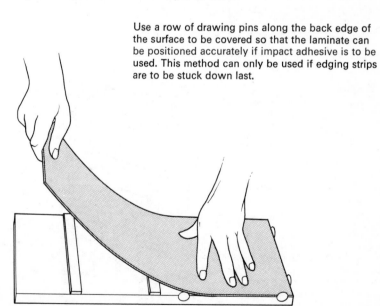

You will find it helps to push drawing pins into the edges of the material being covered so that the edges of the laminate can first be positioned against the undersides of the pin heads.

Or use the lath method for accurate positioning of the laminate. Applying firm hand pressure to the middle of the laminate and working out towards the edges as each lath is removed will ensure that no air bubbles are trapped underneath.

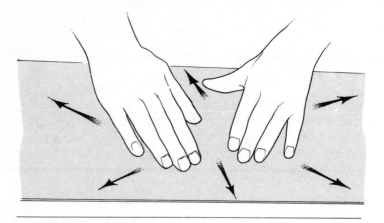

Press the laminate into position forcing any air away from the centre. Then complete the bonding by going over the entire surface tapping a smooth flat wooden block with a hammer.

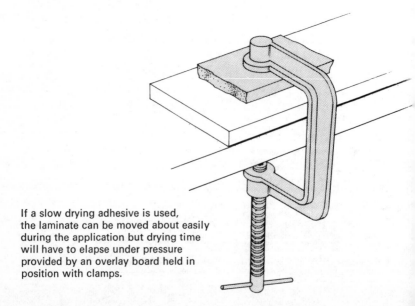

If a slow drying adhesive is used, the laminate can be moved about easily during the application but drying time will have to elapse under pressure provided by an overlay board held in position with clamps.

Finally, complete the bond by running a smooth block of wood all over the surface of the laminate and tapping it firmly with a hammer.

When using a slow drying adhesive, accurate first-time positioning is not necessary as the laminate can be moved about on the surface. While setting, use a board and G cramps to secure the laminate in position.

Many articles (table tops for instance) have raw edges which must also be laminated. Use the same principles as above.

If you prefer, there are ready-made edging strips available at d-i-y shops. These save cutting narrow strips. Obviously, though, it is more economical to use up any waste strips for edges.

Laminate will pull timber or man-made boards out of shape so the reverse side of, say, a door must also be covered in a matching grade of laminate to compensate and prevent this happening.

Plastic coverings

The simplest and cheapest of all the covering materials are the flexible plastics such as Fablon or Contact which can be cut to shape with scissors. The adhesive is already on the back protected by a backing paper which is peeled off and the material smoothed into place. These plastics are available in a range of patterns and colours.

Veneers

A veneer is a thin slice, sold in large sheets, taken from an expensive wood. By using a veneer, a cheap carcase – made of plywood, blockboard or softwood – can be made to look like an expensive piece of furniture.

The surface of the carcase has to be absolutely smooth otherwise the veneer will not stick down properly. This is why man-made boards such as plywood or blockboard are ideal: natural timber can have an undulating surface which is difficult for the beginner to smooth out.

If you do use timber as a base, always lay veneer at right angles to the grain – this prevents cracks developing.

PVA adhesive can be used to stick down veneer though the surface must be scratched first with glasspaper (F2 grade) to make a key for the adhesive.

Cut the veneer to size using a Stanley knife held against a straight-edge. Allow a 12 mm ($\frac{1}{2}$ in) overlap all round which can be trimmed off later.

Spread the glue evenly on the surface, taking special care to cover all edges. Lay the veneer in position and cover it with a sheet of paper. Cover the paper with a 18 mm ($\frac{3}{4}$ in) thick sheet of block-board which is 12 mm ($\frac{1}{2}$ in) larger all round than the veneer. Secure it firmly in position with G cramps. The sheet of paper is needed in case the glue soaks through the veneer and reaches the blockboard.

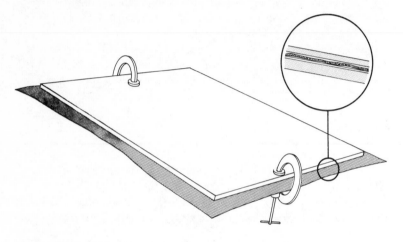

Lay a sheet of brown paper over the veneer once it has been placed onto the glued surface. Clamp an overlay board in position until the adhesive has thoroughly set.

After twenty-four hours, remove the cramps, the blockboard and the protective paper. Turn the panel over so that the veneer is face down on a flat surface. Then trim off the 12 mm ($\frac{1}{2}$ in) surplus using the Stanley knife. This will leave a flush finish at the edges.

There are now two veneering systems sold which avoid the necessity of making a blockboard press to secure the veneer while the glue is setting. The range of finishes is, however, limited.

Handi-veneer can be cut to size with scissors. The adhesive is already on the back. It is activated by laying the veneer in position and smoothing it out with a domestic electric iron.

Point One rollwood veneer is also cut with scissors. A special adhesive is applied to the aluminium foil backing of the veneer and the surface being covered. When the adhesive is nearly dry, the veneer is pressed into place.

Veneer strip which has been coated with adhesive is available in various widths. Simply place in position on a clean surface and rub over with a warm iron to soften the adhesive.

Paint

Paint is commonly used to finish wood or man-made boards because anyone, with care, is able to produce a pleasing, decorative finish in any colour.

Considerable preparation is often needed. If the correct preparatory work is overlooked, the pattern of the grain will show through the paintwork.

Most people use gloss paint, though an eggshell, matt or one of the other popular finishes is quite acceptable if you prefer it. Gloss paint however is more wear-resistant than other types.

First, rub down the suface with glasspaper (0 grade). Work diagonally across the grain initially, then finish in the direction of the grain.

If there are any knots in natural timber, brush over these with a substance called knot stopping. This is a shellac sealer which is readily available at decorating shops. If knots are not sealed they can exude resin which can bleed through the paint causing brown patches on the surface.

The next operation involves working filler (Polyfilla will do) into the surface to leave a smooth finish. If you looked at a magnified picture of grain formation, you would see an undulating surface.

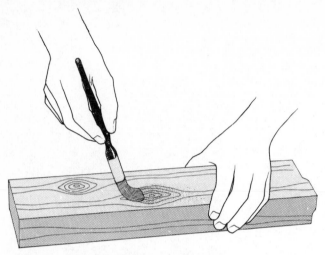

Any live knots in timber should be treated with a brushing application of shellac knotting before proceeding with painting. This will hold back the resin from bleeding through the paint film.

Though a first-class finish is not necessary on, say, a kitchen shelf for storing pots and pans, a display shelf in the living room does need to look really good.

Using a filling knife, press the filler into the surface, working across the grain. Allow twenty-four hours for the filler to harden, then rub down the surface with glasspaper (0 grade) wrapped round a cork or wood block. Repeat this operation, working with the grain.

Use a steel filling knife to press grain filler well into the surface of the timber. Allow thoroughly to harden before rubbing down with a fine glass paper.

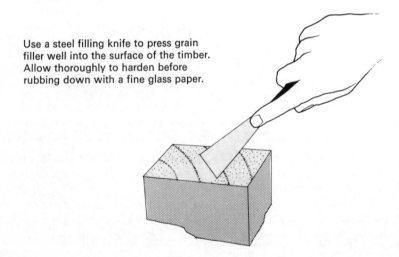

Again allow twenty-four hours before rubbing down with glasspaper.

If you have chosen a gloss of eggshell finish, now apply a coat of primer. Brush on the primer across the grain, then brush diagonally and, finally, finish with the grain.

Apply the correct undercoat for the gloss. It is worth while using a second undercoat after the first has dried, as this will make the gloss finish that much more smooth. Finally, apply the gloss.

Both the undercoat and the gloss should be applied as for primer.

Another worthwhile precaution is to rub down with a rag moistened with methylated spirit immediately before applying primer, undercoat and gloss. This will remove all specks of dust which have settled on the surface.

Some man-made boards have a smooth surface, so filling is not quite so essential. In such cases, an initial rub down with glasspaper is sufficient preparation.

The same application techniques are used for each paint coat – primer, undercoat, and gloss.

Other finishes

Certain finishes are applied to wood to make the grain look more attractive and also to protect and preserve the surface. In this category are French polish, stain, wax polish, varnish, sealer and lacquer.

Before a finish is applied, the grain must be both smooth and clean. Filling the grain with grainfiller makes the surface smooth, and thereafter, easier to dust and keep clean.

Nearly all finishes have to be mixed with a solvent to thin them and make application easier. Methylated spirit, white spirit and cellulose thinners are normal solvents. Follow the manufacturer's instructions closely.

Although a professional would use a smoothing plane followed by glasspaper to achieve a smooth finish, the beginner would be better off omitting the plane stage. This is a skilled operation which if done incorrectly, will leave the surface more uneven than ever. You will gain a satisfactory finish using glasspaper alone, provided that you bought ready-planed timber initially.

If you have an electrical orbital sander or a sander attachment for an electric drill, these will provide an excellent finish with very little effort.

An electric orbital sander is the ideal power tool for providing a really fine finish to a piece of timber.

Glasspaper

Glasspaper comes in grades ranging from fine to coarse. The coarse grains are for the initial smoothing of a really rough surface, the fine grades are used to gain the final, smooth effect.

A cabinet scraper will provide a clean level, smooth surface to timber.

For basic purposes, two of the fine grades will be sufficient. Initially, use 1½ grade (a medium/fine glasspaper); finish off with 0 grade (a fine glasspaper).

Glasspaper is sold in sheets of about 250 mm × 125 mm (10 ins × 5 ins). For economy, cut the sheets into quarters. To avoid scratching the surface, wrap the glasspaper around a wood block and work it in the direction of the grain.

A cabinet scraper will also provide a clean, level, smooth surface on timber. These scrapers are available with throw-away blades. Alternatively, use a piece of saw steel filed down to leave a perfectly square edge.

The next stage is to fill the grain with grainfiller. Again, where wood is to be painted, whether or not you bother filling the grain depends very much on the way it is to be used.

Proprietary grainfillers are available in natural wood shades.

Use a circular motion to work the filler into the grain with a cloth pad or a filling knife. Level it off working in the direction of the grain. Finally, rub down with glasspaper in the direction of the grain before dusting off.

French polish

This gives a mirror-like finish though several coats are needed to produce a reflective surface. The finish will be neither heatproof nor waterproof.

There are various types of French polish but the transparent type gives the clearest and hardest finish. It is bought in liquid form and mixed with a little methylated spirit.

The polish is applied with a pad made by wrapping a piece of clean, white linen around a wad of cotton wool about the size of a golf ball. The pad is called a rubber.

Place the cotton wool in the centre of the linen. Pour enough polish on to the wool to saturate it, then fold the linen as shown overleaf.

The sole of the pear shaped rubber which will contact the surface must be free from wrinkles if an even layer of polish is to be applied.

It is preferable that the rubber is more dry than wet. Too much polish will leave ridges on the surface when the polish has dried. So, before use on the real thing, press the rubber on to a waste piece of wood to remove the excess polish.

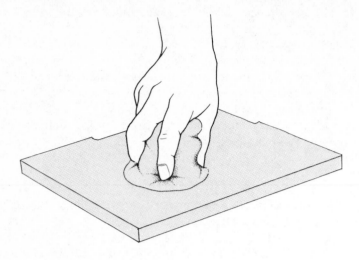

Apply the polish with a small pad formed by wrapping a piece of clean linen around cotton wool.

A few drops of linseed oil on the sole of the rubber will act as a lubricant and make the work easier.

Work the rubber in a loop action. Initially, use light pressure. Gradually increase pressure as the polish is used up. The extra pressure will force the last drop of polish through the rubber.

When dry, open up the rubber and apply more polish to the cotton wool. Again use a few drops of linseed oil on the rubber. Complete the entire surface.

The polish will dry in a few minutes. Between applications, store the rubber in a jam jar with the lid screwed on tightly. This prevents the rubber becoming hard. Finally, thin the remaining polish in the cotton wool by adding methylated spirit, then squeeze out the rubber on to a clean, waste piece of wood until it is nearly dry.

Work the rubber backwards and forwards following the grain. Do not 'scrub' the surface and do not use linseed oil in this final stage. This process will remove any marks left by the rubber. The surface should dry out almost immediately.

Stains

Stains are used to change the colour of timber to a preferred shade. In this way, an inexpensive softwood can be given the colour of an expensive hardwood, such as mahogany or walnut. However, only the colour will be similar. The beautiful grain configuration of an expensive wood cannot be reproduced.

Stains must be covered with a sealer (see page 88), French polish or other finish. This is because the stain, without protection, could fade in places.

Always test the colour of a stain on a similar piece of wood before use so that you know in advance what colour you are going to produce.

There are three types of stain: water, oil and spirit.

Water stains are the best buy for the beginner; they are also the cheapest. They are made by dissolving crystals or powder in water. They have the advantage that if the shade proves to be too dark on the timber, it can be washed back to the desired colour with a wet rag.

Water stains do tend to raise the grain of the wood, so thorough smoothing with glasspaper is essential before they are applied.

Oil stains, though more expensive, are the most popular type. They do not raise the grain and are quick drying. They are sold ready-mixed for use.

Spirit stains dry quickly and are made by dissolving the stain powder in methylated spirits. Bright colours as well as natural wood shades are available. They are often used to tint French polish.

Before applying stain, stick masking tape over the face edges of the worksurface. This will prevent any stain running off the top surface and forming streaks on the face edges.

Use a non-fluffy cloth to apply water stain. Work in the direction of the grain. It is important to work quickly to join up all wet edges before they dry. Avoid going over the same area twice. If you ignore these points, a patchy finish will result.

Remove the masking tape and apply a half-strength coat to the edges. This is necessary because the end grain (seen at the edges) would finish up a darker colour than the surface if a uniform strength stain was applied throughout.

When dry, rub down with 000 grade glasspaper and dust off before applying a sealer, polish or other suitable finish.

Wax polish

This is the easiest form of finish for the amateur to apply successfully: proprietary brands are best for beginners, though enthusiasts often prefer to mix their own wax polish by dissolving beeswax and carnauba wax in white spirit.

Wax polish gives a better sheen to a French polished surface.

It is not advisable to put wax directly on to bare wood as the wax tends to transfer dirt around the pores of the wood leaving a greyish surface colour.

Polyurethane varnish

This gives a hard, transparent finish which has good resistance to water, heat and abrasion. Available in a high gloss and a matt finish, it is likely to darken slightly the colour of the wood. It is often used as a protective coating over wood stain.

Coloured types are available so that the wood can be stained and polished in one operation. However, if the surface is subsequently scratched, the wood will show through in its original colour. At least three coats are needed to obtain a sufficiently thick, protective layer.

There are two types of polyurethane varnish: one pack and two-pack.

The ingredients of the two-pack type have to be mixed together. This type gives a slightly harder finish.

The one-pack type can be applied immediately and is adequate for normal use.

Use a good quality brush to apply the varnish. Brush it out evenly working in the direction of the grain. Finish with light strokes.

As each coat dries, rub it down lightly with glasspaper (grade 0). Dust down the surface before applying the next coat.

Sealers

These give a hardwearing finish which brings out the grain of the wood. Proprietary makes are easy to apply. Just work them into the surface using a clean rag or a brush. Rub down each coat with fine wire wool. The final coat should be thin.

Teak oils also come into the category of sealers; these successfully bring out the colour as well as the grain and can be used effectively on a range of timbers and veneers other than teak.

Cellulose lacquers

Cellulose lacquers are either clear or coloured. They dry to a hard, reasonably heat-resistant finish in about an hour.

The clear types are used mainly on hardwoods. They enhance the colour of the wood and the formation of the grain pattern.

The coloured types are especially suitable for children's toys or things that have to withstand rough treatment.

A single coat will give a matt finish. A further coat will leave a satin finish. A third coat will leave a glossier finish.

Lacquer must not be spread out on the surface like gloss paint. A flowing coat should be applied with the grain using a good quality soft bristle brush. If this is not done, brush marks will show through after the lacquer has dried.

Allow each coat to dry for the recommended time before rubbing down the surface with wire wool (grade 0000). Then dust down and apply the next coat.

Useful Books

The following is a list of titles which provide useful information and guidance for the beginner who has mastered the techniques covered in this book.

A. R. Whittick, *Carpentry and Joinery*, Butterworth Group, 88 Kingsway, London, WC2B 6AB.

Rolf Schutze, *Making Modern Danish Furniture*, Van Nostrand Reinhold Co Ltd, 25/28 Buckingham Gate, London SW1E 6LQ.

Charles Hayward, *Tools for Woodwork* and *The Complete Book of Woodwork*, Evans Brothers (Books) Ltd, Montague House, Russell Square, London WC1B 5BX.

G. W. Endacott, *Woodworking and Furniture Making for the Home*, David and Charles (Holdings) Ltd, South Devon House, Newton Abbot, Devon.

Stanley Book of Designs for Home Storage, Spectator Publications Ltd, 91 St Martin's Lane, London WC2.

Softwood sections in mm (inches in brackets)

Thicknesses	75(3)	100(4)	125(5)	150(6)	Widths 175(7)	200(8)	225(9)	250(10)	300(12)
$16(\frac{5}{8})$	×	×	×	×					
$19(\frac{3}{4})$	×	×	×	×					
$22(\frac{7}{8})$	×	×	×	×					
25(1)	×	×	×	×	×	×	×	×	×
$32(1\frac{1}{4})$	×	×	×	×	×	×	×		
$38(1\frac{1}{2})$	×	×	×	×	×	×	×		
$44(1\frac{3}{4})$	×	×	×	×	×	×	×	×	×
50(2)	×	×	×	×	×	×	×	×	×
$53(2\frac{1}{2})$		×	×	×	×	×	×		
75(3)		×	×	×	×	×	×	×	×
100(4)		×			×		×		×	×
150(6)				×		×			×
200(8)						×			
250(10)								×	
300(12)									×

Softwood lengths (in m)

1·8
2·1
2·4
2·7
3·0
3·3
3·6
3·9
4·2
4·5
4·8
5·1
5·4
5·7
6·0
6·3

Index

Compiled by Susan Kennedy